A PRIEST TO THE TEMPLE

or

THE COUNTRY PARSON

with selected poems

A PRIEST TO THE TEMPLE
or
THE COUNTRY PARSON

with selected poems

GEORGE HERBERT

Edited and Introduced by
Ronald Blythe

CANTERBURY
PRESS
Norwich

Introduction © Ronald Blythe 2003

First published in 2003 by the Canterbury Press Norwich
(a publishing imprint of
Hymns Ancient & Modern Limited, a registered charity)
St Mary's Works, St Mary's Plain,
Norwich, Norfolk NR3 3BH

www.scm-canterburypress.co.uk

Second impression 2007

British Library Cataloguing in Publication data

A catalogue record for this book is available
from the British Library

ISBN 978-1-85311-532-5

Typeset by Rowland Phototypesetting Ltd,
Bury St Edmunds, Suffolk
Printed and bound in Great Britain by
MPG Books Ltd, Bodmin, Cornwall

CONTENTS

[v]

INTRODUCTION

THIS powerful little 'Rule' for the village clergy was
published in 1652, almost twenty years after *The Temple*,
George Herbert's collected poems. The latter had been
handed to Arthur Woodnoth by the poet as he lay dying
in Bemerton Rectory with the instruction to take them to
his master Nicholas Ferrar at Little Gidding, who was to
burn them if he did not find them worthy to keep. Ferrar
recognised a Christian masterpiece and *The Temple* – from
Psalm 29 'In his Temple doth every man speak of his
honour' – appeared within weeks of Herbert's death on 1
March 1633. But there were other writings. And so there
arrived by a now celebrated author, *Herbert's Remains. Or,
Sundry Pieces of that Sweet Singer of the Temple, Mr George
Herbert*. They included *A Priest to the Temple: or, The
Country Parson*, a small book consisting of thirty-seven
chapters, some of them hardly more than long para-
graphs, but all of them pithy with a kind of commanding
advice. All of the chapters except two begin with 'The
Countrey Parson . . .' There follows, not a polite request
or a hope, but a requirement. The parson will do this, he
will be that. As his Lord's representative in the parish he
has no leeway. Since, as we know, George Herbert's
experience of being a country clergyman was brief in the
extreme, probably no more than two years when he
wrote this strict book, we might wonder at his nerve. But
as we also know – it is a famous story – his own ex-
perience called for protestation. Having given up for

ordination so many things to which his aristocratic back-
ground entitled him – a grand role at Cambridge, the
Court, a seat in Parliament – he had asked for the living
of Fuggleston-cum-Bemerton near Salisbury, only to
discover their churches tumbledown and their rectory
uninhabitable. Equally ruined was his prebendal church
at Leighton Bromswold near Little Gidding. And, we
realise, in much the same state as many a country living
up and down the land.

Had he not died just before his fortieth birthday from
consumption, Herbert's *The Country Parson* would have
been his clarion call to the rural Church of England to re-
order itself and become worthy of its Lord. Behind its
many injunctions lie his pain that things have come to
such a state. Buildings apart, and no one more than he
was to re-teach the sacredness which existed in church
architecture, the country people themselves were un-
visited, untaught, even shunned by the clergy, who found
them too 'low' to know. By his insistent use of the title
'Parson', Herbert reminds each priest that he is *the*
Person in each little community, the one man to whom
all have access for their needs, spiritual and practical,
altar and hearth, body and soul. An impossible task, of
course, yet none must dodge the attempt. Trying to be
Christ-like is what makes many a minister succeed. The
twenty-first-century reader of *The Country Parson* will at
first be caught up in seventeenth-century prose, though
not for long. George Herbert's Rule itself soon becomes
quite toughly adaptable to modern parish duties,
although, as with the demands of all literary saints, com-
mon sense tells us how far we can go in carrying them
out. In housekeeping terms – 'who sweeps a room, as for

thy laws' – he would be enchanted by the physical state of the average country church today, each one so perfectly kept, flowers and all. But his severe requirements for the clergy still hold up an ideal. They have to do what Christ did. They must aspire to his teachings, to his actions, nothing less. 'Nothing is little in God's service', he tells some priest who senses the trivial nature of much which he is called to do. He has to be full of charity, 'It is his dominant element. His giving is in effect a sermon'. But then in Herbertian terms so is his every action and as we read on we wonder how anyone is able to endure the exposure which a village priest suffers, even now. Although as close to his flock 'as if he had begot the whole parish', he remains an outsider by virtue of his calling. All these years later we are made to recognise an isolation which R. S. Thomas would prove to be indestructible.

George Herbert's short life at Bemerton was an open book to the three hundred or so agriculturists who became his parishioners in April 1630. One might call it a field day for Anglicanism. He had married Jane Danvers his stepfather's cousin a few months earlier and was about to mend not only his 'pittiful little chappell', as John Aubrey called it, but unknown to himself many of the gaps in Anglicanism. He was ill, with tuberculosis 'working like a mole' inside him. He and his wife and their servants walked across the lane twice a day to say their prayers. On Thursdays he walked via the water meadows to Salisbury Cathedral to sing in the choir. The poetry of *The Temple* was being written. He played his lute. Christ accompanied him everywhere and in everything. His happiness and privilege overwhelmed him. And thus it was that he wrote a Rule for those who, like him, sought for what he knew to be the best of all lives, that of a country parson. No one was to tell him that he was a great religious poet or that anyone outside his parish and aristocratic circle would remember him. Where he was concerned his end was a desired simplicity and obscurity. Just his initials on the church wall.

But then a month or so hence the poems of *The Temple* burst out with that Herbertian cry, 'My God and King!', and with them a new understanding of priesthood in the English Church. Two decades later came a textbook for the clergy, and for us, living so much later, a vivid account of what it was like to run a parish in the post-Reformation years when so much had been changed, destroyed or abandoned, and many priests had lost their confidence, and the old parish churches themselves seemed to have lost their meaning. Tragically by 1652, when *The Country Parson* was published, these ancient buildings were to suffer a further 'cleansing' by having their window imagery smashed. When George Herbert wrote:

> A man that looks on glasse,
>   On it may stay his eye;
> Or, if he pleaseth, through it passe,
>   And then the heav'n espie.

he was describing the iconic purpose of stained glass. Its pictures carried the eye to the divine realities which lay behind them. Or through them. Today, none of his requirements are more carried out to the letter than those in Chapter XIII.

The Countrey Parson hath a speciall care of his Church, that all things there be decent, and befitting his Name by which it is called [St Andrew at Bemerton]. Therefore first he takes order, that all things be in good repair; as walls plaistered, windows glazed, floore paved, seats whole, firm, and uniform, especially that the Pulpit, and Desk, and Communion Table, and Font be as they ought, for those great duties that are performed in them. Secondly, that the Church be swept, and kept cleane without dust, or Cobwebs, and at great festivalls strawed, and stuck with boughs, and perfumed with incense.

There are to be seemly carpets, fine linen, books and, high up, painted texts. All this we now easily comprehend. Enter any village church and one could not encounter better godly housekeeping. What may have slipped our notice is the status of its incumbent, which is what this little book is all about. We can imagine a young ordinand reading it and finding what is expected of him quite overwhelming. But Herbert says very few things about priestly weakness and inadequacy, and even less about scandal. His purpose is to remind the humblest village clergyman that he is Christ's right-hand man in the parish. Being this, he says, will inevitably set you apart from other men and make your life hard. Yet you must bridge this gulf and come close in Christ's love to every individual in your care.

And then we get – with still a surprising forcefulness from a writer whose background was so patrician and intellectual, who when at Cambridge drew attention to his lineage by wearing fine clothes, whose mother was at the centre of London literary life and whose brothers were at Court – as true and perceptive an account of ordinary country folk as they tilled the land as can be found at that period, accurate vignettes of them which go straight to the heart. If there is anything which proves George Herbert's total transition from what he had been to what he became at Bemerton it is this 'seeing' of his flock. The Country Parson is never to avert his gaze or withold his friendship from the worst who may be sharing his patch. They are his family in Christ and as such must be taught, fed and nursed. The parsonage itself must be a kind of open house, a holy model for the poorest cottage. He must have a knowledge of farming and must actually teach gardening. For Herbert gardens were dispensaries as well as earthly paradises, places of healing and delight. The Parson is to make the 'garden a shop' for 'home-bred medicines' and all Herbert's pleasure in flowers and expertise in herbs makes these pages especially memorable. He was himself a considerable dietitian and he believed that every country clergyman – and his wife – should know about home cures. As he practised what he preached, or wrote, we have to witness revolutionary changes at Bemerton during that short incumbency; changes which, given the popularity of *The Temple* and *The Country Parson* during the seventeenth century, would have travelled across Britain.

> Herbs gladly cure our flesh, because they
>   Find their acquaintance there.

As with the Ferrars at Little Gidding, Herbert is keen on literacy and his Country Parson must educate. 'If he finds some one borrowing a Bible he gives him one for his own'. He must catechise, 'building up knowledge until it becomes a spiritual temple', and must be careful when catechising not to have a pupil learning 'by rote, as parrats, without even piercing into the sense of it'. And he the parson-teacher must learn from his parishioners what a plough, hatchet, bushel are, why boys go 'piping and dancing', and why 'country people are much addicted to old customs'. The Parson must love what they love and understand what they understand. And they, in their way, must gain some of his knowledge of religion.

The Country Parson reveals both the routine and the aspiration of a priest's life during the nervous years preceding the Civil War, but which, due to Herbert's genius and personal example, were to make their mark for generations to come. He remains enormously influential. The reader may have to update his sociology and translate his beautiful English, but his spiritual meaning grows brighter by the day. He had a passion for aphorisms and proverbs and in his witty fashion he adds to them, such as when he writes that luxury is 'a very visible sin', and that the priest has to be 'a tracker of God's ways'. Here and there we come across that authoritarianism which caused quarrels to break out between parishioners and priest, 'At Baptism he admits no vain or idle names but such as are usual and accustomed.' But then we have his radical view, 'Evident miseries have a natural privilege and exemption from all Law'. As now, he finds that 'Country people are full of petty injustices'. He has no patience with idleness, 'Even in Paradise man had a calling'. He has the poet's ear for ancient sayings. Every time a candle is brought into a room the Bemerton people say, 'God send us the light of heaven'. *The Country Parson* is part handbook, part village recording and very much part autobiography. It should be read in tandem with Herbert's poems and 'heard' when singing his hymns. These are his thoughts and hopes, his teachings and prayers for the Church of England.

WILLIAM DYCE

The cover picture, *George Herbert at Bemerton*, was painted by the Scottish artist William Dyce R.A. in 1861. It shows the poet in his rectory garden by the river Nadder, neatly dressed in his cassock and with a finger holding the place in his prayer-book. The spire of Salisbury Cathedral is in the background. Fishing-tackle by a tree reminds us that Izaak Walton, author of *The Compleat Angler* (1653), was Herbert's first biographer. William Dyce had some claim to be called the first Pre-Raphaelite. He was a High Churchman and, as well as an artist, an authority on seventeenth-century church music and the decorator of All Saints, Margaret Street. He was also an expert designer of stained glass. He died in 1864.

A PRIEST TO THE TEMPLE

or

THE COUNTRY PARSON

THE COUNTRY PARSON

HIS CHARACTER AND RULE OF LIFE

The Authour to the Reader

BEING desirous (thorow the Mercy of God) to please
Him, for whom I am, and live, and who giveth mee my
Desires and Performances; and considering with my self,
That the way to please him, is to feed my Flocke dili-
gently and faithfully, since our Saviour hath made that
the argument of a Pastour's love, I have resolved to set
down the Form and Character of a true Pastour, that I
may have a Mark to aim at: which also I will set as
high as I can, since hee shoots higher that threatens the
Moon, then[1] hee that aims at a Tree. Not that I think,
if a man do not all which is here expressed, hee
presently sinns, and displeases God, but that it is a good
strife to go as farre as wee can in pleasing of him, who
hath done so much for us. The Lord prosper the inten-
tion to my selfe, and others, who may not despise my
poor labours, but add to those points, which I have
observed, untill the Book grow to a compleat Pastorall.

GEO. HERBERT

1632

[1] i.e. ' than ', and so frequently through the book.

CHAPTER I

Of a Pastor

A PASTOR is the Deputy of Christ for the reducing[1] of Man to the Obedience of God. This definition is evident, and containes the direct steps of Pastorall Duty and Auctority. For first, Man fell from God by disobedience. Secondly, Christ is the glorious instrument of God for the revoking[2] of Man. Thirdly, Christ being not to continue on earth, but after hee had fulfilled the work of Reconciliation, to be received up into heaven, he constituted Deputies in his place, and these are Priests. And therefore St. *Paul* in the beginning of his Epistles, professeth this: and in the first to the *Colossians* plainly avoucheth, that he *fils up that which is behinde of the afflictions of Christ in his flesh, for his Bodie's sake, which is the Church*. Wherein is contained the complete definition of a Minister. Out of this Chartre of the Priesthood may be plainly gathered both the Dignity thereof, and the Duty: The Dignity, in that a Priest may do that which Christ did, and by his auctority, and as his Viceregent. The Duty, in that a Priest is to do that which Christ did, and after his manner, both for Doctrine and Life.

[1] i.e. ' leading back '.
[2] i.e. ' recalling '.

CHAPTER II

Their Diversities

Of Pastors (intending mine own Nation only, and also therein setting aside the Reverend Prelates of the Church, to whom this discourse ariseth not) some live in the Universities, some in Noble houses, some in Parishes residing on their Cures. Of those that live in the Universities, some live there in office, whose rule is that of the Apostle; *Rom.* 12.6. *Having gifts differing, according to the grace that is given to us, whether prophecy, let us prophecy according to the proportion of faith; or ministry, let us wait on our ministring; or he that teacheth, on teaching, &c. he that ruleth, let him do it with diligence, &c.* Some in a preparatory way, whose aim and labour must be not only to get knowledg, but to subdue and mortifie all lusts and affections: and not to think, that when they have read the Fathers, or Schoolmen, a Minister is made, and the thing done. The greatest and hardest preparation is within: For, *Unto the ungodly, saith God, Why dost thou preach my Laws, and takest my Covenant in thy mouth? Psal.* 50.16. Those that live in Noble Houses are called Chaplains, whose duty and obligation being the same to the Houses they live in, as a Parsons to his Parish, in describing the one (which is indeed the bent of my Discourse) the other will be manifest. Let not Chaplains think themselves so free, as *many of them do,* and because they have different Names, think their Office different. Doubtlesse they are Parsons of the families they live in, and are entertained to that end, either by an open, or implicite Covenant. Before they are in Orders, they may be received for Companions, or discoursers; but after a man is once Minister, he cannot agree to come into any house, where he shall not exercise what he is, unlesse he forsake his plough, and look back. Wherfore they are not to be over-submissive, and base, but to keep up with the Lord and Lady of the house, and to preserve a boldness with them and all, even so farre as reproofe to their very face, when occasion cals, but seasonably and discreetly. They who do not thus, while they remember their earthly Lord, do much forget their heavenly; they wrong the Priesthood, neglect their duty, and shall be so farre from that which they seek with their over-submissivenesse, and cringings, that they shall ever be despised. They who for the hope of promotion neglect any necessary admonition, or reproofe, sell (with *Judas*) their Lord and Master.

CHAPTER III

The Parson's Life

The Countrey Parson is exceeding exact in his Life, being holy, just, prudent, temperate, bold, grave in all his wayes. And because the two highest points of Life, wherein a Christian is most seen, are Patience, and Mortification; Patience in regard of afflictions, Mortification in regard of lusts and affections, and the stupifying and deading of all the clamorous powers of the soul, therefore he hath throughly studied these, that he may be an absolute Master and commander of himself, for all the purposes which God hath ordained him. Yet in these points he labours most in those things which are most apt to scandalize his Parish. And first, because Countrey people live hardly, and therefore as feeling their own sweat, and consequently knowing the price of mony, are offended much with any, who by hard usage increase their travell, the Countrey Parson is very circumspect in avoiding all coveteousnesse, neither being greedy to get, nor nigardly to keep, nor troubled to lose any worldly wealth; but in all his words and actions slighting, and disesteeming it, even to a wondring, that the world should so much value wealth, which in the day of wrath hath not one dramme of comfort for us. Secondly, because Luxury is a very visible sinne, the Parson is very carefull to avoid all the kinds thereof, but especially that of drinking, because it is the most popular vice; into which if he come, *he prostitutes himself* both to shame, and sin, and by having *fellowship, with the unfruitfull works of darknesse,* he disableth himself of authority *to reprove them* : For sins make all equall, whom they finde together; and then they are worst, who ought to be best. Neither is it for the servant of Christ to haunt Innes, or Tavernes, or Ale-houses, *to the dishonour of his person and office.* The Parson doth not so, but orders his Life in such a fashion, that when death takes him, as the Jewes and *Judas* did Christ, he may say as He did, *I sate daily with you teaching in the Temple.* Thirdly, because Countrey people (as indeed

[7]

all honest men) do much esteem their word, it being the Life of buying, and selling, and dealing in the world; therfore the Parson is very strict in keeping his word, though it be to his own hinderance, as knowing, that if he be not so, he wil quickly be discovered, and disregarded: neither will they beleeve him in the pulpit, whom they cannot trust in his Conversation. As for oaths, and apparell, the disorders thereof are also very manifest. The Parsons yea is yea and nay nay; and his apparrell plaine, but reverend, and clean, without spots, or dust, or smell; the purity of his mind breaking out, and dilating it selfe even to his body, cloaths, and habitation.

CHAPTER IV

The Parson's Knowledg

The Countrey Parson is full of all knowledg. They say, it is an ill Mason that refuseth any stone: and there is no knowledg, but, in a skilfull hand, serves either positively as it is, or else to illustrate some other knowledge. He condescends even to the knowledge of tillage, and pastorage, and makes great use of them in teaching, because people by what they understand, are best led to what they understand not. But the chief and top of his knowledge consists in the book of books, the storehouse and magazene of life and comfort, the holy Scriptures. There he sucks, and lives. In the Scriptures hee findes four things; Precepts for Life, Doctrines for knowledge, Examples for illustration, and Promises for comfort: There he hath digested severally. But for the understanding of these; the means he useth are first, a holy Life, remembring what his Master saith, that *if any do Gods will, he shall know of the Doctrine, John* 7, and assuring himself, that wicked men, however learned, do not know the Scriptures, because they feel them not, and because they are not understood but with the same spirit that writ them. The second means is prayer, which if it be necessary even in temporall things, how much more in things of another world, where the well is deep, and we have nothing of our selves to draw with? Wherefore he ever begins the reading of the Scripture with some short inward ejaculation, as, *Lord, open mine eyes, that I may see the wondrous things of thy Law, &c.* The third means is a diligent Collation of Scripture with Scripture. For all Truth being consonant to it self, and all being penn'd by one and the self-same Spirit, it cannot be, but that an industrious, and judicious comparing of place with place must be a singular help for the right understanding of the Scriptures. To this may be added the consideration of any text with the coherence thereof, touching what goes before, and what follows after, as also the scope of the Holy Ghost. When the Apostles would have called down fire from Heaven, they were reproved, as ignorant of what spirit they were. For the Law required one thing, and the Gospel another: yet as diverse, not as repugnant: therefore the spirit of both is to be considered, and weighed. The fourth means are Commenters and Fathers, who have handled the places controverted, which the Parson by no means refuseth. As he doth not so study others, as to neglect the grace of God in himself, and what the Holy Spirit teacheth him; so doth he assure himself, that God in all ages hath had his servants, to whom he hath revealed his Truth, as well as to him; and that as one Countrey doth not bear all things, that there may be a Commerce; so neither hath God opened, or will open all to one, that there may be a traffic in knowledg between the servants of God, for the planting both of love, and humility. Wherfore he hath one Comment at least upon every book of Scripture, and ploughing with this, and his own meditations, he enters into the secrets of God treasured in the holy Scripture.

CHAPTER V

The Parson's Accessary Knowledges

The Countrey Parson hath read the Fathers also, and the Schoolmen, and the later Writers, or a good proportion of all, out of all which he hath compiled a book, and body of Divinity, which is the storehouse of his Sermons, and which he preacheth all his Life; but diversely clothed, illustrated, and inlarged. For though the world is full of such composures, yet every mans own is fittest, readyest, and most savory to him. Besides, this being to be done in his younger and preparatory times, it is an honest joy ever after to looke upon his well spent houres. This Body he made by way of expounding the Church Catechisme, to which all divinity may easily be reduced. For it being indifferent in it selfe to choose any Method, that is best to be chosen, of which there is likelyest to be most use. Now Catechizing being a work of singular, and admirable benefit to the Church of God, and a thing required under Canonicall obedience, the expounding of our Catechisme must needs be the most usefull forme. Yet hath the Parson, besides this laborious work, a slighter form of Catechizing, fitter for country people; according as his audience is, so he useth one, or other; or sometimes both, if his audience be intermixed. He greatly esteemes also of cases of conscience, wherein he is much versed. And indeed, herein is the greatest ability of a Parson to lead his people exactly in the wayes of Truth, so that they neither decline to the right hand, nor to the left. Neither let any think this a slight thing. For every one hath not digested, when it is a sin to take something for mony lent, or when not; when it is a fault to discover anothers fault, or when not; *when the affections of the soul in desiring and procuring increase of means, or honour, be a sin of covetousnes or ambition, and when not; when the appetites of the body in eating, drinking, sleep, and the pleasure that comes with sleep, be sins of gluttony, drunkenness, sloath, lust, and when not,* and so in many circumstances of actions. Now if a shepherd know not which grass will bane, or which not, how is he fit to be a shepherd? Wherefore the Parson hath throughly canvassed al the particulars of humane actions, at least all those which he observeth are most incident to his Parish.

CHAPTER VI

The Parson praying

The Countrey Parson, when he is to read divine services, composeth himselfe to all possible reverence; lifting up his heart and hands, and eyes, and using all other gestures which may expresse a hearty, and unfeyned devotion. This he doth, first, as being truly touched and amazed with the Majesty of God, before whom he then presents himself; yet not as himself alone, but as presenting with himself the whole Congregation, whose sins he then beares, and brings with his own to the heavenly altar to be bathed, and washed in the sacred Laver of Christs blood. Secondly, as this is the true reason of his inward feare, so he is content to expresse this outwardly to the utmost of his power; that being first affected himself, hee may affect also his people, knowing that no Sermon moves them so much to a reverence, which they forget againe, when they come to pray, as a devout behaviour in the very act of praying. Accordingly his voyce is humble, his words treatable, and slow; yet not so slow neither, as to let the fervency of the supplicant hang and dy between speaking, but with a grave livelinesse, between fear and zeal, pausing yet pressing, he performes his duty. Besides his example, he having often instructed his people how to carry themselves in divine service, exacts of them all possible reverence, by no means enduring either talking, or sleep-

ing, or gazing, or leaning, or halfe-kneeling, or any un-
dutifull behaviour in them, but causing them, when
they sit, or stand, or kneel, to do all in a strait, and
steady posture, as attending to what is done in the
Church, and every one, man, and child, answering aloud
both Amen, and all other answers, which are on the
Clerks and peoples part to answer; which answers also
are to be done not in a hudling, or slubbering fashion,
gaping, or scratching the head, or spitting even in the
midst of their answer, but gently and pausably, thinking
what they say; so that while they answer, *As it was in
the beginning, &c.* they meditate as they speak, that God
hath ever had his people, that have glorified him as wel
as now, and that he shall have so for ever. And the like
in other answers. This is that which the Apostle cals a
reasonable service, *Rom.* 12, when we speak not as
Parrats, without reason, or offer up such sacrifices as
they did of old, which was of beasts devoyd of reason;
but when we use our reason, and apply our powers to
the service of him, that gives them. If there be any of
the gentry or nobility of the Parish, who sometimes
make it a piece of state not to come at the beginning of
service with their poor neighbours, but at mid-prayers,
both to their own loss, and of theirs also who gaze upon
them when they come in, and neglect the present service
of God, he by no means suffers it, but after divers gentle
admonitions, if they persevere, he causes them to be pre-
sented: or if the poor Church-wardens be affrighted
with their greatness, notwithstanding his instruction
that they ought not to be so, but even to let the world
sinke, so they do their duty; he presents them himself,
only protesting to them, that not any ill will draws him

[13]

to it, but the debt and obligation of his calling, being to
obey God rather then men.

CHAPTER VII

The Parson preaching

The Countrey Parson preacheth constantly, the pulpit
is his joy and his throne: if he at any time intermit, it
is either for want of health, or against some great Festi-
vall, that he may the better celebrate it, or for the
variety of the hearers, that he may be heard at his
returne more attentively. When he intermits, he is ever
very well supplyed by some able man who treads in
his steps, and will not throw down what he hath built;
whom also he intreats to press some point, that he him-
self hath often urged with no great success, that so in
the mouth of two or three witnesses the truth may be
more established. When he preacheth, he procures
attention by all possible art, both by earnestnesse of
speeche, it being naturall to men to think, that where
is much earnestness, there is somewhat worth hearing;
and by a diligent, and busy cast of his eye on his
auditors, with letting them know, that he observes who
marks, and who not; and with particularizing of his
speech now to the younger sort, then to the elder, now
to the poor, and now to the rich. This is for you, and
This is for you; for particulars ever touch, and awake
more than generalls. Herein also he serves himselfe
of[1] the judgements of God, as of those of antient times,

[1] i.e. 'makes use of'.

[14]

so especially of the late ones; and of those most, which are nearest to his Parish; for people are very attentive at such discourses, and think it behoves them to be so, when God is so neer them, and even over their heads. Sometimes he tells them stories, and sayings of others, according as his text invites him; for them also men heed, and remember better then exhortations; which though earnest, yet often dy with the Sermon, especially with Countrey people; which are thick, and heavy, and hard to raise to a poynt of Zeal, and fervency, and need a mountaine of fire to kindle them; but stories and sayings they will well remember. He often tels them, that Sermons are dangerous things, that none goes out of Church as he came in, but either better, or worse; that none is careless before his Judg, and that the word of God shal judge us. By these and other means the Parson procures attention; but the character of his Sermon is Holiness; he is not witty, or learned, or eloquent, but Holy. A Character, that *Hermogenes*[1] never dream'd of, and therefore he could give no precepts thereof. But it is gained, first, by choosing texts of Devotion, not Controversie, moving and ravishing texts, whereof the Scriptures are full. Secondly, by dipping, and seasoning all our words and sentences in our hearts, before they come into our mouths, truly affecting, and cordially expressing all that we say; so that the auditors may plainly perceive that every word is hart-deep. Thirdly, by turning often, and making many Apostrophes to God, as, Oh Lord blesse my people, and teach them this point; or, Oh my Master, on whose errand I come, let

---

[1] A Roman philosopher who wrote about the ' characters ', or characteristics, of good oratory.

me hold my peace, and doe thou speak thy selfe; for thou art Love, and when thou teachest, all are Scholers. Some such irradiations scatteringly in the Sermon, carry great holiness in them. The Prophets are admirable in this. So *Isa.* 64. *Oh that thou would'st rent the Heavens, that thou wouldst come down, &c.* And *Jeremy*, Chapt. 10, after he had complained of the desolation of *Israel*, turnes to God suddenly, *Oh Lord, I know that the way of man is not in himself, &c.* Fourthly, by frequent wishes of the peoples good, and joying therein, though he himself were with Saint *Paul* even sacrificed upon the service of their faith. For there is no greater sign of holinesse, then the procuring, and rejoycing in anothers good. And herein St. *Paul* excelled in all his Epistles. How did he put the *Romans* in all his prayers? *Rom.* 1.9. And ceased not to give thanks for the *Ephesians*, *Eph.* 1.16. And for the *Corinthians*, *chap.* 1.4. And for the *Philippians* made request with joy, *ch.* 1.4. And is in contention for them whither to live, or dy; be with them, or Christ, *verse* 23, which, setting aside his care of his Flock, were a madnesse to doubt of. What an admirable Epistle is the second to the *Corinthians*? how full of affections? he joyes, and he is sorry, he grieves, and he gloryes, never was there such care of a flock expressed, save in the great shepherd of the fold, who first shed teares over *Jerusalem*, and afterwards blood. Therefore this care may be learn'd there, and then woven into Sermons, which will make them appear exceeding reverend, and holy. Lastly, by an often urging of the presence, and majesty of God, by these, or such like speeches. Oh let us all take heed what we do, God sees us, he sees whether I speak as I ought, or you hear as you ought, he sees hearts as we see faces: he is among us; for if we be here, hee must be here, since we are here by him, and without him could not be here. Then turning the discourse to his Majesty, And he is a great God, and terrible, as great in mercy, so great in judgement: There are but two devouring elements, fire, and water, he hath both in him; *His voyce is as the sound of many waters, Revelations* 1. And he himselfe *is a consuming fire, Hebrews* 12. Such discourses shew very Holy. The Parsons Method in handling of a text consists of two parts; first, a plain and evident declaration of the meaning of the text; and secondly, some choyce Observations drawn out of the whole text, as it lyes entire, and unbroken in the Scripture it self. This he thinks naturall, and sweet, and grave. Whereas the other way of crumbling a text into small parts, as, the Person speaking, or spoken to, the subject, and object, and the like, hath neither in its sweetnesse, nor gravity, nor variety, since the words apart are not Scripture, but a dictionary, and may be considered alike in all the Scripture. The Parson exceeds not an hour in preaching, because all ages have thought that a competency, and he that profits not in that time, will lesse afterwards, the same affection which made him not profit before, making him then weary, and so he grows from not relishing, to loathing.

CHAPTER VIII

The Parson on Sundays

The Country Parson, as soon as he awakes on
Sunday morning, presently falls to work, and seems to
himselfe so as a Market-man is, when the Market day
comes, or a shopkeeper, when customers use to come
in. His thoughts are full of making the best of the day,
and contriving it to his best gaines. To this end, besides
his ordinary prayers, he makes a peculiar one for a
blessing on the exercises of the day, That nothing befall
him unworthy of that Majesty before which he is to
present himself, but that all may be done with reverence
to his glory, and with edification to his flock, humbly
beseeching his Master, that how or whenever he punish
him, it be not in his Ministry: then he turnes to request
for his people, that the Lord would be pleased to sanc-
tifie them all, that they may come with holy hearts, and
awfull mindes into the Congregation, and that the good
God would pardon all those, who come with lesse pre-
pared hearts then they ought. This done, he sets himself
to the Consideration of the duties of the day, and if
there be any extraordinary addition to the customary
exercises, either from the time of the year, or from the
State, or from God by a child born, or dead, or any other
accident, he contrives how and in what manner to
induce it to the best advantage. Afterwards when the
hour calls, with his family attending him, he goes to

Church, at his first entrance *humbly adoring, and worshipping the invisible majesty, and presence of Almighty God,* and blessing the people either openly, or to himselfe. Then having read divine Service twice fully, and preached in the morning, and catechized in the afternoone, he thinks he hath in some measure, according to poor, and fraile man, discharged the publick duties of the Congregation. The rest of the day he spends either in reconciling neighbours that are at variance, or in visiting the sick, or in exhortations to some of his flock by themselves, whom his Sermons cannot, or doe not reach. And every one is more awaked, when we come, and say, *Thou art the man.* This way he findes exceeding usefull, and winning; and these exhortations he cals his privy purse, even as Princes have theirs, besides their publick disbursments. At night he thinks it a very fit time, both sutable to the joy of the day, and without hinderance to publick duties, either to entertaine some of his neighbours, or to be entertained of them, where he takes occasion to discourse *of such things as are both profitable, and pleasant, and to raise up their mindes to apprehend Gods good blessing to our Church, and State; that order is kept in the one, and peace in the other, without disturbance, or interruption of publick divine offices.* As he opened the day with prayer, so he closeth it, humbly beseeching the Almighty to pardon and accept our poor services, and to improve them, that we may grow therein, and that our feet may be like hindes feet ever climbing up higher, and higher unto him.

CHAPTER IX

The Parson's state of Life

The Country Parson considering that virginity is a higher state then Matrimony, and that the Ministry requires the best and highest things, is rather unmarryed, then married. But yet as the temper of his body may be, or as the temper of his Parish may be, where he may have occasion to converse with women, and that among suspicious men, *and other like circumstances considered,* he is rather married then unmarried. Let him communicate the thing often by prayer unto God, and as his grace shall direct him, so let him proceed. If he be unmarried, and keepe house, he hath not a woman in his house, but findes opportunities of having his meat dress'd and other services done by men-servants at home, and his linnen washed abroad. If he be unmarryed, and sojourne, he never talkes with any woman alone, but in the audience of others, and that seldom, and then also in a serious manner, never jestingly or sportfully. *He is very circumspect in all companyes, both of his behaviour, speech, and very looks, knowing himself to be both suspected, and envyed. If he stand steadfast in his heart, having no necessity, but hath power over his own will, and hath so decreed in his heart, that he will keep himself a virgin, he spends his dayes in fasting and prayer, and blesseth God for the gift of continency, knowing that it can no way be pre-*

served, but only by those means, by which at first it
was obtained. He therefore thinkes it not enough for
him to observe the fasting dayes of the Church, and the
dayly prayers enjoyned him by auctority, which he
observeth out of humble conformity, and obedience; but
adds to them, out of choice and devotion, some other
dayes for fasting, and hours for prayers; and by these
hee keeps his body tame, serviceable, and healthfull; and
his soul fervent, active, young, and lusty as an eagle.
He often readeth the Lives of the Primitive Monks,
Hermits, and Virgins, and wondreth not so much at
their patient suffering and cheerfull dying under perse-
cuting Emperours, (though that indeed be very admir-
able) as at their daily temperance, abstinence, watchings,
and constant prayers, and mortifications in the times
of peace and prosperity. To put on the profound
humility, and the exact temperance of our Lord Jesus,
with other exemplary vertues of that sort, and to keep
them on in the sunshine, and noone of prosperity, he
findeth to be as necessary, and as difficult at least, as to
be cloathed with perfect patience, and Christian forti-
tude in the cold midnight stormes of persecution and
adversity. He keepeth his watch and ward, night and
day against the proper and peculiar temptations of his
state of Life, which are principally these two, Spirituall
pride, and Impurity of heart: against these ghostly
enemies he girdeth up his loynes, keepes the imagination
from roving, puts on the whole Armour of God, and by
the vertue of the shield of faith, he is not afraid of the
pestilence that walketh in darknesse, [carnall impurity,]
nor of the sicknesse that destroyeth at noone day,
[Ghostly pride and self-conceite.] Other temptations he

*hath, which, like mortall enemies, may sometimes dis-
quiet him likewise; for the humane soule being bounded,
and kept in, in her sensitive faculty, will runne out more
or lesse in her intellectuall. Originall concupisence is
such an active thing, by reason of continuall inward,
or outward temptations, that it is ever attempting, or
doing one mischief or other. Ambition, or untimely
desire of promotion to an higher state, or place, under
colour of accommodation, or necessary provision, is a
common temptation to men of any eminency, especially
being single men. Curiosity in prying into high specu-
lative and unprofitable questions, is another great
stumbling block to the holinesse of Scholars. These and
many other spirituall wickednesses in high places doth
the Parson fear, or experiment, or both; and that much
more being single, then if he were marryed; for then
commonly the stream of temptations is turned another
way, into Covetousness, Love of pleasure, or ease, or
the like. If the Parson be unmarryed, and means to con-
tinue so, he doth at least, as much as hath been said.
If he be marryed, the choyce of his wife was made
rather by his eare, then by his eye; his judgement, not
his affection found a fit wife for him, whose humble,
and liberall disposition he preferred before beauty,
riches, or honour. He knew that (the good instrument
of God to bring women to heaven) a wise and loving
husband could out of humility, produce any speciall
grace of faith, patience, meeknesse, love, obedience, &c.
and out of liberality, make her fruitfull in all good
works. As hee is just in all things, so is he to his wife
also, counting nothing so much his owne, as that he
may be unjust unto it. Therefore he gives her respect*

[22]

both afore her servants, and others, and halfe at least of the government of the house, reserving so much of the affaires, as serve for a diversion for him; yet never so giving over the raines, but that he sometimes looks how things go, demanding an account, but not by the way of an account. And this must bee done the oftner, or the seldomer, according as hee is satisfied of his Wifes discretion.

CHAPTER X

The Parson in his house

The Parson is very exact in the governing of his house, making it a copy and modell for his Parish. He knows the temper, and pulse of every person in his house, and accordingly either meets with their vices, or advanceth their vertues. His wife is either religious, or night and day he is winning her to it. In stead of the qualities of the world, he requires onely three of her; first, a trayning up of her children and mayds in the fear of God, with prayers, and catechizing, and all religious duties. Secondly, a curing, and healing of all wounds and sores with her owne hands; which skill either she brought with her, or he takes care she shall learn it of some religious neighbour. Thirdly, a providing for her family in such sort, as that neither they want a competent sustentation, nor her husband be brought in debt. His children he first makes Christians, and then Commonwealths-men; the one he owes to his heavenly Countrey, the other to his earthly, having no title to either, except he do good to both. Therefore having seasoned them with all Piety, not only of words in praying, and reading; but in actions, in visiting other sick children, and tending their wounds, and sending his charity by them to the poor, and somtimes giving them a little mony to do it of themselves, that they get a delight in it, and enter favour with God, who weighs even childrens actions, I *King*. 14.12, 13. He afterwards turnes his care to fit all their dispositions with some calling, not sparing the eldest, but giving him the prerogative of his Fathers profession, which happily for his other children he is not able to do. Yet in binding them prentices (in case he think fit to do so) he takes care not to put them into vain trades, and unbefitting the reverence of their Fathers calling, such as are tavernes for men, and lace-making for women; because those trades, for the most part, serve but the vices and vanities of the world, which he is to deny, and not augment. However, he resolves with himself never to omit any present good deed of charity, in consideration of providing a stock for his children; but assures himselfe, that mony thus lent to God, is placed surer for his childrens advantage, then if it were given to the Chamber of *London*. Good deeds, and good breeding, are his two great stocks for his children; if God give any thing above those, and not spent in them, he blesseth God, and lays it out as he sees cause. His servants are all religious, and were it not his duty to have them so, it were his profit, for none are so well served, as by religious servants, both because they do best, and because what they do, is blessed, and prospers. After

[24]

religion, he teacheth them, that three things make a compleate servant, Truth, and Diligence, and Neatnesse, or Cleanlinesse. Those that can read, are allowed times for it, and those that cannot, are taught; for all in his house are either teachers or learners, or both, so that his family is a Schoole of Religion, and they all account, that to teach the ignorant is the greatest almes. Even the wals are not idle, but something is written, or painted there, which may excite the reader to a thought of piety, especially the 101 *Psalm*, which is expressed in a fayre table, as being the rule of a family. And when they go abroad, his wife among her neighbours is the beginner of good discourses, his children among children, his servants among other servants; so that as in the house of those that are skill'd in Musick, all are Musicians; so in the house of a Preacher, all are preachers. He suffers not a ly or equivocation by any means in his house, but counts it the art, and secret of governing to preserve a directnesse, and open plainnesse in all things; so that all his house knowes, that there is no help for a fault done, but confession. He *himselfe*, or his *Wife*, takes account of Sermons, and how every one profits, comparing this yeer with the last : and besides the common prayers of the family, he straitly requires of all to pray by themselves before they sleep at night, and stir out in the morning, and knows what prayers they say, and till they have learned them, makes them kneel by him; esteeming that this private praying is a more voluntary act in them, then when they are called to others prayers, and that, which when they leave the family, they carry with them. He keeps his servants between love, and fear, according as hee findes

them; but generally he distributes it thus, To his
Children he shewes more love then terrour, to his ser-
vants more terrour then love; but an old good servant
boards[1] a child. The furniture of his house is very plain,
but clean, whole, and sweet, as sweet as his garden
can make; for he hath no mony for such things, charity
being his only perfume, which deserves cost when he
can spare it. His fare is plain, and common, but whole-
some, what hee hath, is little, but very good; it con-
sisteth most of mutton, beefe, and veal, if he addes any
thing for a great day, or a stranger, his garden or
orchard supplyes it, or his barne, and back-side : he goes
no further for any entertainment, lest he goe into the
world, esteeming it absurd, that he should exceed, who
teacheth others temperance. But those which his home
produceth, he refuseth not, as coming cheap, and easie,
and arising from the improvement of things, which
otherwise would be lost. Wherein he admires and imi-
tates the wonderfull providence and thrift of the great
householder of the world : for there being two things,
which as they are, are unuseful to man, the one for
smalnesse, as crums, and scattered corn, and the like;
the other for the foulnesse, as wash, and durt, and
things thereinto fallen; God hath provided Creatures for
both; for the first, Poultry; for the second, swine. These
save man the labour, and doing that which either he
could not do, or was not fit for him to do, by taking
both sorts of food into them, do as it were dresse and
prepare both for man in themselves, by growing them
selves fit for his table. The Parson in his house observes
fasting dayes; and particularly, as Sunday is his day of

[1] i.e. comes near to the status of a child.

joy, so Friday his day of Humiliation, which he cele-
brates not only with abstinence of diet, but also of com-
pany, recreation, and all outward contentments; and
besides, with confession of sins, and all acts of Mortifi-
cation. Now fasting dayes containe a treble obligation;
first, of eating lesse that day, then on other dayes;
secondly, of eating no pleasing, or over-nourishing
things, as the Israelites did eate sowre herbs: Thirdly,
of eating no flesh, which is but the determination of the
second rule by Authority to this particular. The two
former obligations are much more essentiall to a true
fast, then the third and last; and fasting dayes were fully
performed by keeping of the two former, had not
Authority interposed: so that to eat little, and that
unpleasant, is the naturall rule of fasting, although it be
flesh. For since fasting in Scripture language is an afflict-
ing of our souls, if a peece of dry flesh at my table be
more unpleasant to me, then some fish there, certainly
to eat the flesh, and not the fish, is to keep the fasting
day naturally. And it is observable, that the prohibiting
of flesh came from hot Countreys, where both flesh
alone, and much more with wine, is apt to nourish more
then in cold regions, and where flesh may be much
better spared, and with more safety then elsewhere,
where both the people and the drink being cold and
flegmatick, the eating of flesh is an antidote to both. For
it is certaine, that a weak stomack being prepossessed
with flesh, shall much better brooke and bear a draught
of beer, then if it had taken before either fish, or rootes,
or such things; which will discover it selfe by spitting,
and rheume, or flegme. To conclude, the Parson, if he
be in full health, keeps the three obligations, eating fish,

or roots, and that for quantity little, for quality un-pleasant. If his body be weak and obstructed, as most Students are, he cannot keep the last obligation, nor suffer others in his house that are so, to keep it; but only the two former, which also in diseases of exinani-tion (as consumptions) must be broken : For meat was made for man, not man for meat. To all this may be added, not for emboldening the unruly, but for the com-fort of the weak, that not onely sicknesse breaks these obligations of fasting, but sicklinesse also. For it is as unnatural to do any thing, that leads me to a sicknesse, to which I am inclined, as not to get out of that sick-nesse, when I am in it, by any diet. One thing is evident, that an English body, and a Students body, are two great obstructed vessels, and there is nothing that is food, and not phisick, which doth lesse obstruct, then flesh moderately taken; as being immoderately taken, it is exceeding obstructive. And obstructions are the cause of most diseases.

CHAPTER XI

The Parson's Courtesie

The Countrey Parson owing a debt of Charity to the poor, and of Courtesie to his other parishioners, he so distinguisheth, that he keeps his money for the poor, and his table for those that are above Alms. Not but that the poor are welcome also to his table, whom he sometimes purposely takes home with him, setting them close by him, and carving for them, both for his own humility, and their comfort, who are much cheered with such friendliness. But since both is to be done, the better sort invited, and meaner relieved, he chooseth rather to give the poor money, which they can better employ to their own advantage, and sutably to their needs, then so much given in meat at dinner. Having then invited some of his Parish, hee taketh his times to do the like to the rest; so that in the compasse of the year, hee hath them all with him, because countrey people are very observant of such things, and will not be perswaded, but being not invited, they are hated. Which perswasion the Parson by all means avoyds, knowing that where there are such conceits, there is no room for his doctrine to enter. Yet doth hee oftenest invite those, whom hee sees take best courses, that so both they may be encouraged to persevere, and others spurred to do well, that they may enjoy the like courtesie. For though he desire, that all should live well, and vertuously, not for any reward of his, but for vertues sake; yet that will not be so: and therefore as God, although we should love him onely for his own sake, yet out of his infinite pity hath set forth heaven for a reward to draw men to Piety, and is content, if at least so, they will become good: So the Countrey Parson, who is a diligent observer, and tracker of Gods wayes, sets up as many encouragements to goodnesse as he can, both in honour, and profit, and fame; that he may, if not the best way, yet any way, make his Parish good.

CHAPTER XII

The Parson's Charity

The Countrey Parson is full of Charity; it is his pre-dominant element. For many and wonderfull things are spoken of thee, thou great Vertue. To Charity is given the covering of sins, I *Pet.* 4.8, and the forgivenesse of sins, *Matthew* 6.14. *Luke* 7.47. The fulfilling of the Law, *Romans* 13.10. The life of faith, *James* 2.26. The blessings of this life, *Proverbs* 22.9. *Psalm* 41.2. And the reward of the next, *Matth.* 25.35. In brief, it is the body of Religion, *John* 13.35. And the top of Christian vertues, I *Corin.* 13. Wherefore all his works rellish of Charity. When he riseth in the morning, he bethinketh himselfe what good deeds he can do that day, and presently doth them; counting that day lost, wherein he hath not exercised his Charity. He first considers his own Parish, and takes care, that there be not a begger, or idle person in his Parish, but that all bee in a competent way of getting their living. This he effects either by bounty, or perswasion, or by authority, making use of that excellent statute, which bindes all Parishes to maintain their own. If his Parish be rich, he exacts this of them; if poor, and he able, he easeth them therein. But he gives no set pension to any; for this in time will lose the name and effect of Charity with the poor people, though not with God: for then they will reckon upon it, as on a debt; and if it be taken away, though justly, they will murmur, and repine as much, as he that is disseized of his own inheritance. But the Parson having a double aime, and making a hook of his Charity, causeth them still to depend on him; and so by continuall, and fresh bounties, unexpected to them, but resolved to himself, hee wins them to praise God more, to live more religiously, and to take more paines in their vocation, as not knowing when they shal be relieved; which otherwise they would reckon upon, and turn to idlenesse. Besides this generall provision, he hath other times of opening his hand; as at great Festivals, and Communions; not suffering any that day that hee receives, to want a good meal suting to the joy of the occasion. But specially, at hard times, and dearths, he even parts his Living, and life among them, giving some corn outright, and selling other at under rates; and when his own stock serves not, working those that are able to the same charity, still pressing it in the pulpit, and out of the pulpit, and never leaving them, till he obtaine his desire. Yet in all his Charity, he distinguisheth, giving them most, who live best, and take most paines, and are most charged : So is his charity in effect a Sermon. After the consideration of his own Parish, he inlargeth himself, if he be able, to the neighbour-hood; for that also is some kind of obligation; so doth he also to those at his door, whom God puts in his way, and makes his neighbours. But these he helps not without some testimony, except the evidence of the misery bring testimony with it. For though these testimonies also may be falsifyed, yet considering that the Law allows these in case they be true, but allows by no means to give without testimony, as he obeys Authority

[31]

in the one, so that being once satisfied, he allows his Charity some blindnesse in the other; especially, since of the two commands, we are more injoyned to be charitable, then wise. But evident miseries have a naturall priviledge, and exemption from all law. Whenever hee gives any thing, and sees them labour in thanking of him, he exacts of them to let him alone, and say rather, God be praised, God be glorified; that so the thanks may go the right way, and thither onely, where they are onely due. So doth hee also before giving make them say their Prayers first, or the Creed, and ten Commandments, and as he finds them perfect, rewards them the more. For other givings are lay, and secular, but this is to give like a Priest.

CHAPTER XIII

The Parson's Church

The Countrey Parson hath a speciall care of his Church, that all things there be decent, and befitting his Name by which it is called. Therefore first he takes order, that all things be in good repair; as walls plaistered, windows glazed, floore paved, seats whole, firm, and uniform, especially that the Pulpit, and Desk, and Communion Table, and Font be as they ought, for those great duties that are performed in them. Secondly, that the Church be swept, and kept cleane without dust, or Cobwebs, and at great festivalls strawed, and stuck with boughs, and perfumed with incense. Thirdly, That there be fit, and proper texts of Scripture every where painted, and that all the painting be grave, and reverend, not with light colours, or foolish anticks. Fourthly, That all the books appointed by Authority be there, and those not torne, or fouled, but whole and clean, and well bound; and that there be a fitting, and sightly Communion Cloth of *fine linnen, with an handsome, and seemly Carpet of good and costly Stuffe, or Cloth, and all kept sweet and clean, in a strong and decent chest, with a Chalice, and Cover, and a Stoop, or Flagon; and a Bason for Almes and offerings; besides which, he hath a Poor-Mans Box conveniently seated, to receive the charity of well minded people, and to lay up treasure for the sick and needy*. And all this he doth, not as out of necessity, or as putting a holiness in the things, but as desiring to keep the middle way between superstition, and slovenlinesse, and as following the Apostles two great and admirable Rules in things of this nature : The first whereof is, *Let all things be done decently, and in order* : The second, *Let all things be done to edification,* I *Cor.* 14. For these two rules comprize and include the double object of our duty, God, and our neighbour; the first being for the honour of God; the second for the benefit of our neighbor. So they excellently score out the way, and fully, and exactly contain, even in externall and indifferent things, what course is to be taken; and put them to great shame, who deny the Scripture to be perfect.

CHAPTER XIV

The Parson in Circuit

The Countrey Parson upon the afternoons in the weekdays, takes occasion sometimes to visite in person, now one quarter of his Parish, now another. For there he shall find his flock most naturally as they are, wallowing in the midst of their affairs: whereas on Sundays it is easie for them to compose themselves to order, which they put on as their holy-day cloathes, and come to Church in frame, but commonly the next day put off both. When he comes to any house, first he blesseth it, and then as hee finds the persons of the house imployed, so he formes his discourse. Those that he findes religiously imployed, hee both commends them much, and furthers them when hee is gone, in their imployment; as if hee findes them reading, hee furnisheth them with good books; if curing poor people, hee supplies them with Receipts, and instructs them further in that skill, shewing them how acceptable such works are to God, and wishing them ever to do the Cures with their own hands, and not to put them over to servants. Those that he finds busie in the works of their calling, he commendeth them also: for it is a good and just thing for every one to do their own busines. But then he admonisheth them of two things; first, that they dive not too deep into worldly affairs, plunging themselves over head and eares into carking, and caring; but that

[34]

they so labour, as neither to labour anxiously, nor dis-
trustfully, nor profanely. Then they labour anxiously,
when they overdo it, to the loss of their quiet, and
health: then distrustfully, when they doubt Gods
providence, thinking that their own labour is the cause
of their thriving, as if it were in their own hands to
thrive, or not to thrive. *Then they labour profanely,
when they set themselves to work like brute beasts,
never raising their thoughts to God, nor sanctifying
their labour with daily prayer; when on the Lords day
they do unnecessary servile work, or in time of divine
service on other holy days, except in the cases of
extreme poverty, and in the seasons of Seed-time, and
Harvest.* Secondly, he adviseth them so to labour for
wealth and maintenance, as that they make not that the
end of their labour, but that they may have where-
withall to serve God the better, and to do good deeds.
After these discourses, if they be poor and needy, whom
he thus finds labouring, he gives them somewhat; and
opens not only his mouth, but his purse to their relief,
that so they go on more cheerfully in their vocation,
and himself be ever the more welcome to them. Those
that the Parson findes idle, or ill imployed, he chides not
at first, for that were neither civill, nor profitable; but
always in the close, before he departs from them: yet
in this he distinguisheth; for if he be a plaine country-
man, he reproves him plainly; for they are not sensible
of finenesse: if they be of higher quality, they commonly
are quick, and sensible, and very tender of reproof: and
therefore he lays his discourse so, that he comes to the
point very leasurely, and oftentimes, as *Nathan* did, in
the person of another, making them to reprove them-

selves. However, one way or other, he ever reproves them, that he may keep himself pure, and not be intangled in others sinnes. Neither in this doth he forbear, though there be company by : for as when the offence is particular, and against mee, I am to follow our Saviours rule, and to take my brother aside, and reprove him; so when the offence is publicke, and against God, I am then to follow the Apostles rule, I *Timothy* 5.20. and to *rebuke openly* that which is done openly. Besides these occasionall discourses, the Parson questions what order is kept in the house, as about prayers morning and evening on their knees, reading of Scripture, catechizing, singing of Psalms at their work, and on holy days; who can read, who not; and sometimes he hears the children read himselfe, and blesseth them, encouraging also the servants to learn to read, and offering to have them taught on holy-dayes by his servants. If the Parson were ashamed of particularizing in these things, hee were not fit to be a Parson : but he holds the Rule, that Nothing is little in Gods service : If it once have the honour of that Name, it grows great instantly. Wherfore neither disdaineth he to enter into the poorest Cottage, though he even creep into it, and though it smell never so lothsomly. For both God is there also, and those for whom God dyed : and so much the rather doth he so, as his accesse to the poor is more comfortable, then to the rich; and in regard of himselfe, it is more humiliation. These are the Parsons generall aims in his Circuit; but with these he mingles other discourses for conversation sake, and to make his higher purposes slip the more easily.

[36]

CHAPTER XV

The Parson Comforting

The Countrey Parson, when any of his cure is sick,
or afflicted with losse of friend, or estate, or any ways
distressed, fails not to afford his best comforts, and
rather goes to them, then sends for the afflicted, though
they can, and otherwise ought to come to him. To this
end he hath throughly digested all the points of con-
solation, as having continuall use of them, such as are
from God's generall providence extended even to lillyes;
from his particular, to his Church; from his promises,
from the examples of all Saints, that ever were; from
Christ himself, perfecting our Redemption no other
way, then by sorrow; from the Benefit of affliction,
which softens, and works the stubborn heart of man;
from the certainty both of deliverance, and reward, if
we faint not; from the miserable comparison of the
moment of griefs here with the weight of joyes here-
after. *Besides this, in his visiting the sick, or otherwise
afflicted, he followeth the Churches counsell, namely,
in perswading them to particular confession, labouring
to make them understand the great good use of this
antient and pious ordinance, and how necessary it is in
some cases: he also urgeth them to do some pious charit-
able works, as a necessary evidence and fruit of their
faith, at that time especially: the participation of the
holy Sacrament, how comfortable, and Soveraigne a*

Medicine it is to all sin-sick souls; what strength, and joy, and peace it administers against all temptations, even to death it selfe, he plainly, and generally intimateth to the disaffected, or sick person, that so the hunger and thirst after it may come rather from themselves, then from his perswasion.

CHAPTER XVI

The Parson a Father

The Countrey Parson is not only a father to his flock, but also professeth himselfe throughly of the opinion, carrying it about with him as fully, as if he had begot his whole Parish. And of this he makes great use. For by this means, when any sinns, he hateth him not as an officer, but pityes him as a Father : and even in those wrongs which either in tithing, or otherwise are done to his owne person, hee considers the offender as a child, and forgives, so hee may have any signe of amendment; so also when after many admonitions, any continue to be refractory, yet hee gives him not over, but is long before hee proceede to disinheriting, or perhaps never goes so far; knowing, that some are called at the eleventh houre, and therefore hee still expects, and waits, least hee should determine Gods houre of coming; which as hee cannot, touching the last day, so neither touching the intermediate days of Conversion.

CHAPTER XVII

The Parson in Journey

The Countrey Parson, when a just occasion calleth him out of his Parish (which he diligently, and strictly weigheth, his Parish being all his joy, and thought) leaveth not his Ministry behind him; but is himselfe where ever he is. Therefore those he meets on the way he blesseth audibly, and with those he overtakes or that overtake him, hee begins good discourses, such as may edify, interposing sometimes some short, and honest refreshments, which may make his other discourses more welcome, and lesse tedious. And when he comes to his Inn, he refuseth not to joyne, that he may enlarge the glory of God, to the company he is in, by a due blessing of God for their safe arrival, and saying grace at meat, and at going to bed by giving the Host notice, that he will have prayers in the hall, wishing him to informe his guests thereof, that if any be willing to partake, they may resort thither. The like he doth in the morning, using pleasantly the outlandish proverb, that *Prayers and Provender never hinder journey.* When he comes to any other house, where *his kindred, or other relations give him any authority over the Family,* if hee be to stay for a time, hee considers diligently the state thereof to Godward, and that in two points: First, what disorders there are either in Apparell, or Diet, or too open a Buttery,[1] or reading vain books, or swearing, or

---

[1] A storeroom for provisions.

breeding up children to no Calling, but in idleness, or the like. Secondly, what means of Piety, whether daily prayers be used, Grace, reading of Scriptures, and other good books, how *Sundayes, holy-days, and fasting days* are kept. And accordingly, as he finds any defect in these, hee first considers with himselfe, what kind of remedy fits the temper of the house best, and then hee faithfully, and boldly applyeth it; yet seasonably, and discreetly, by taking aside the Lord or Lady, or *Master* and *Mistres* of the house, and shewing them cleerly, that they respect them most, who wish them best, and that not a desire to meddle with others affairs, but the earnestnesse to do all the good he can, moves him to say thus and thus.

CHAPTER XVIII

The Parson in Sentinell

The Countrey Parson, where ever he is, keeps Gods watch; that is, there is nothing spoken, or done in the Company where he is, but comes under his Test and censure. If it be well spoken, or done, he takes occasion to commend, and enlarge it; if ill, he presently lays hold of it, least the poyson steal into some young and unwary spirits, and possesse them even before they themselves heed it. But this he doth discretely, with mollifying, and suppling words; This was not so well said, as it might have been forborn; We cannot allow this: or else if the thing will admit interpretation; Your meaning is not thus, but thus; or, So farr indeed what you say is true, and well said; but this will not stand. This is called keeping Gods watch, when the baits which the enemy lays in company, are discovered and avoyded : This is to be on Gods side, and be true to his party. Besides, if he perceive in company any discourse tending to ill, either by the wickedness or quarrelsomnesse thereof, he either prevents it judiciously, or breaks it off seasonably by some diversion. Wherein a pleasantness of disposition is of great use, men being willing to sell the interest, and ingagement of their discourses for no price sooner, then that of mirth; whither the nature of man, loving refreshment, gladly betakes it selfe, even to the losse of honour.

CHAPTER XIX

The Parson in reference

The Countrey Parson is sincere and upright in all his relations. And first, he is just to his Countrey; as when he is set at an armour, or horse, he borrowes them not to serve the turne, nor provides slight, and unusefull, but such as are every way fitting to do his Countrey true and laudable service, when occasion requires. To do otherwise, is deceit; and therefore not for him, who is hearty, and true in all his wayes, as being the servant of him, in whom there was no guile. Likewise in any other Countrey-duty, he considers what is the end of any Command, and then he suits things faithfully according to that end. Secondly, he carryes himself very respectively, as to all the Fathers of the Church, so especially to his Diocesan, honouring him both in word and behaviour, and resorting unto him in any difficulty, either in his studies or in his Parish. He observes Visitations, and being there, makes due use of them, as of Clergy councels, for the benefit of the Diocese. And therefore before he comes, having observed some defects in the Ministry, he then either in Sermon, if he preach, or at some other time of the day, propounds among his Brethren what were fitting to be done. Thirdly, he keeps good Correspondence with all the neighbouring Pastours round about him, performing for them any Ministeriall office, which is not to the prejudice of his own Parish. Likewise he welcomes to his house any Minister, how poor or mean soever, with as joyfull a countenance, as if he were to entertain some great Lord. Fourthly, he fulfills the duty, and debt of neighbourhood to all the Parishes which are neer him. For the Apostles rule *Philip* 4. being admirable, and large, that *we should do whatsoever things are honest, or just, or pure, or lovely, or of good report, if there be any vertue, or any praise;* and Neighbourhood being ever reputed, even among the Heathen, as an obligation to do good, rather then to those that are further, where things are otherwise equall, therefore he satisfies this duty also. Especially, if God have sent any calamity either by fire, or famine, to any neighbouring Parish, then he expects no Briefe;[1] but taking his Parish together *the next Sunday*, or *holy-day*, and exposing to them the uncertainty of humane affairs, none knowing whose turne may be next, and

[1] i.e. does not wait for an official letter asking for a collection.

then when he hath affrighted them with this, exposing
the obligation of Charity, and Neighbour-hood, he first
gives himself liberally, and then incites them to give;
making together a summe either to be sent, or, which
were more comfortable, all together choosing some fitt
day to carry it themselves, and cheere the Afflicted. So,
if any neighbouring village be overburdened with poore,
and his owne lesse charged, hee findes some way of
releeving it, and reducing the Manna, and bread of
Charity to some equality, representing to his people,
that the Blessing of God to them ought to make them
the more charitable, and not the lesse, lest he cast their
neighbours poverty on them also.

CHAPTER XX

The Parson in Gods stead

The Countrey Parson is in Gods stead to his Parish,
and dischargeth God what he can of his promises.
Wherefore there is nothing done either wel or ill,
whereof he is not the rewarder, or punisher. If he
chance to finde any reading in anothers Bible, he provides
him one of his own. If he finde another giving a poor
man a penny, he gives him a tester for it, if the giver
be fit to receive it; or if he be of a condition above such
gifts, he sends him a good book, or easeth him in his
Tithes, telling him when he hath forgotten it, This I
do, because at such, and such a time you were charit-
able. This is in some sort a discharging of God; as

concerning this life, who hath promised, that Godlinesse shall be gainfull: but in the other God is his own immediate paymaster, rewarding all good deeds to their full proportion. *The Parsons punishing of sin and vice, is rather by withdrawing his bounty and courtesie from the parties offending, or by private, or publick reproof,. as the case requires, then by causing them to be presented, or otherwise complained of. And yet as the malice of the person, or hainousness of the crime may be, he is carefull to see condign punishment inflicted, and with truly godly zeal, without hatred to the person, hungreth and thirsteth after righteous punishment of unrighteousnesse. Thus both in rewarding vertue, and in punishing vice, the Parson endeavoureth to be in Gods stead, knowing that Countrey people are drawne, or led by sense, more then by faith, by present rewards, or punishments, more then by future.*

CHAPTER XXI

The Parson Catechizing

The Countrey Parson values Catechizing highly: for there being three points of his duty, the one, to infuse a competent knowledge of salvation in every one of his Flock; the other, to multiply, and build up this knowledge to a spirituall Temple; the third, to inflame this knowledge, to presse, and drive it to practice, turning it to reformation of life, by pithy and lively exhortations; Catechizing is the first point, and but by Catechizing,

the other cannot be attained. Besides, whereas in
Sermons there is a kinde of state, in Catechizing there
is an humblenesse very sutable to Christian regeneration,
which exceedingly delights him as by way of exercise
upon himself, and by way of preaching to himself, for
the advancing of his own mortification; for in preaching
to others, he forgets not himself, but is first a Sermon
to himself, and then to others; growing with the growth
of his Parish. He useth, and preferreth the ordinary
Church-Catechism, partly for obedience to Authority,
partly for uniformity sake, that the same common
truths may be every where professed, especially since
many remove from Parish to Parish, who like Christian
Souldiers are to give the word, and to satisfie the Con-
gregation by their Catholick answers. He exacts of all
the Doctrine of the Catechisme; of the younger sort,
the very words; of the elder, the substance. Those
he Catechizeth publickly, these privately, giving age
honour, according to the Apostles rule, I *Tim.* 5.1. He
requires all to be present at Catechizing: First, for the
authority of the work; Secondly, that Parents, and
Masters, as they hear the answers prove, may when they
come home, either commend or reprove, either reward
or punish. Thirdly, that those of the elder sort, who are
not well grounded, may then by an honourable way
take occasion to be better instructed. Fourthly, that
those who are well grown in the knowledg of Religion,
may examine their grounds, renew their vowes, and by
occasion of both, inlarge their meditations. When once
all have learned the words of the Catechisme, he thinks
it the most usefull way that a Pastor can take, to go
over the same, but in other words: for many say the

Catechisme by rote, as parrats, without ever piercing
into the sense of it. In this course the order of the
Catechisme would be kept, but the rest varyed: as thus,
in the Creed: How came this world to be as it is? Was
it made, or came it by chance? Who made it? Did you
see God make it? Then are there some things to be
beleeved that are not seen? Is this the nature of beliefe?
Is not Christianity full of such things, as are not to be
seen, but beleeved? You said, God made the world; Who
is God? And so forward, requiring answers to all these,
and helping and cherishing the Answerer, by making
the Question very plaine with comparisons, and making
much even of a word of truth from him. This order
being used to one, would be a little varyed to another.
And this is an admirable way of teaching, wherein the
Catechized will at length finde delight, and by which
the Catechizer, if he once get the skill of it, will draw
out of ignorant and silly souls, even the dark and deep
points of Religion. *Socrates* did thus in Philosophy, who
held that the seeds of all truths lay in every body, and
accordingly by questions well ordered he found Philo-
sophy in silly Trades-men. That position will not hold
in Christianity, because it contains things above nature:
but after that the Catechisme is once learn'd, that which
nature is towards Philosophy, the Catechism is towards
Divinity. To this purpose, some dialogues in *Plato* were
worth the reading, where the singular dexterity of
Socrates in this kind may be observed, and imitated.
Yet the skill consists but in these three points: First, an
aim and mark of the whole discourse, whither to drive
the Answerer, which the Questionist must have in his
mind before any question be propounded, upon which

and to which the questions are to be chained. Secondly, a most plain and easie framing the question, even containing in vertue the answer also, especially to the more ignorant. Thirdly, when the answerer sticks, an illustrating the thing by something else, which he knows, making what hee knows to serve him in that which he knows not: As, when the Parson once demanded after other questions about mans misery; since man is so miserable, what is to be done? And the answerer could not tell; He asked him again, what he would do, if he were in a ditch? This familiar illustration made the answer so plaine, that he was even ashamed of his ignorance; for he could not but say, he would hast out of it as fast as he could. Then he proceeded to ask, whether he could get out of the ditch alone, or whether he needed a helper, and who was that helper. This is the skill, and doubtlesse the Holy Scripture intends thus much, when it condescends to the naming of a plough, a hatchet, a bushell, leaven, boyes piping and dancing; shewing that things of ordinary use are not only to serve in the way of drudgery, but to be washed, and cleansed, and serve for lights even of Heavenly Truths. This is the Practice which the Parson so much commends to all his fellow-labourers; the secret of whose good consists in this, that at Sermons, and Prayers, men may sleep or wander; but when one is asked a question, he must discover what he is. This practice exceeds even Sermons in teaching: but there being two things in Sermons, the one Informing, the other Inflaming; as Sermons come short of questions in the one, so they farre exceed them in the other. For questions cannot inflame or ravish, that must be done by a set, and laboured, and continued speech.

CHAPTER XXII

The Parson in Sacraments

The Countrey Parson being to administer the Sacraments, is at a stand with himself, how or what behaviour to assume for so holy things. Especially at Communion times he is in a great confusion, as being not only to receive God, but to break, and administer him. Neither findes he any issue in this, but to throw himself down at the throne of grace, saying, Lord, thou knowest what thou didst, when thou appointedst it to be done thus; therefore doe thou fulfill what thou didst appoint; for thou art not only the feast, but the way to it. At Baptisme, being himselfe in white, he requires the presence of all, and Baptizeth not willingly, but on Sundayes, or great dayes. Hee admits no vaine or idle names, but such as are usuall and accustomed. Hee says that prayer with great devotion, where God is thanked for calling us to the knowledg of his grace, Baptisme being a blessing, that the world hath not the like. He willingly and cheerfully crosseth the child, and thinketh the Ceremony not onely innocent, but reverend. He instructeth the God-fathers, and God-mothers, that it is no complementall or light thing to sustain that place, but a great honour, and no less burden, as being done both in the presence of God, and his Saints, and by way

[48]

of undertaking for a Christian soul. He adviseth all to
call to minde their Baptism often; for if wise men have
thought it the best way of preserving a state to reduce
it to its principles by which it grew great; certainly, it
is the safest course for Christians also to meditate on
their Baptisme often (being the first step into their great
and glorious calling) and upon what termes, and with
what vowes they were Baptized. At the times of the
Holy Communion, he first takes order with the Church-
Wardens, that the elements be of the best, not cheape,
or course, much lesse ill-tasted, or unwholsome.
Secondly, hee considers and looks into the ignorance,
or carelessness of his flock, and accordingly applies him-
selfe with Catechizings, and lively exhortations, not on
the Sunday of the Communion only (for then it is too
late) but the Sunday, or Sundayes before the Com-
munion, or on the Eves of all those dayes. If there be
any, who having not received yet, are to enter into this
great work, he takes the more pains with them, that
hee may lay the foundation of future Blessings. The
time of every ones first receiving is not so much by
yeers, as by understanding: particularly, the rule may
be this: When any one can distinguish the Sacra-
mentall from common bread, knowing the Institution,
and the difference, hee ought to receive, of what age
soever. Children and youths are usually deferred too
long, under pretence of devotion to the Sacrament, but
it is for want of Instruction; their understandings being
ripe enough for ill things, and why not then for better?
But Parents, and Masters should make hast in this, as
to a great purchase for their children, and servants;
which while they deferr, both sides suffer; the one, in

wanting many excitings of grace; the other, in being worse served and obeyed. The saying of the Catechism is necessary, but not enough; because to answer in form may still admit ignorance : but the Questions must be propounded loosely and wildely, and then the Answerer will discover what hee is. Thirdly, For the manner of receiving, as the Parson useth all reverence himself, so he administers to none but to the reverent. The Feast indeed requires sitting, because it is a Feast; but man's unpreparednesse asks kneeling. Hee that comes to the Sacrament, hath the confidence of a Guest, and hee that kneels, confesseth himself an unworthy one, and therefore differs from other Feasters : but hee that sits, or lies, puts up to an Apostle : Contentiousnesse in a feast of Charity is more scandall then any posture. Fourthly, touching the frequency of the Communion, the Parson celebrates it, if not duly once a month, yet at least five or six times in the year; as, at Easter, Christmasse, Whit-suntide, afore and after Harvest, and the beginning of Lent. And this hee doth, not onely for the benefit of the work, but also for the discharge of the Church-wardens, who being to present all that receive not thrice a year; if there be but three Communions, neither can all the people so order their affairs as to receive just at those times, nor the Church-Wardens so well take notice who receive thrice, and who not.

CHAPTER XXIII

The Parson's Completenesse

The Countrey Parson desires to be all to his Parish, and not only a Pastour, but a Lawyer also, and a Phisician. Therefore hee endures not that any of his Flock should go to Law; but in any Controversie, that they should resort to him as their Judge. To this end, he hath gotten to himself some insight in things ordinarily incident and controverted, by experience, and by reading some initiatory treatises in the Law, with *Daltons* Justice of Peace, and the Abridgements of the Statutes, as also by discourse with men of that profession, whom he hath ever some cases to ask, when he meets with them; holding that rule, that to put men to discourse of that, wherin they are most eminent, is the most gainfull way of Conversation. Yet when ever any controversie is brought to him, he never decides it alone, but sends for three or four of the ablest of the Parish to hear the cause with him, whom he makes to deliver their opinion first; out of which he gathers, in case he be ignorant himself, what to hold; and so the thing passeth with more authority, and lesse envy. In judging, he followes that, which is altogether right; so that if the poorest man of the Parish detain but a pin unjustly from the richest, he absolutely restores it as a Judge; but when he hath so done, then he assumes the Parson, and exhorts to Charity. Neverthelesse, there may happen somtimes some cases, wherein he chooseth to permit his Parishioners rather to make use of the Law, then himself: As in cases of an obscure and dark nature, not easily determinable by Lawyers themselves; or in cases of high consequence, as establishing of inheritances: or Lastly, when the persons in difference are of a contentious disposition, and cannot be gained, but that they still fall from all compromises that have been made. But then he shews them how to go to Law, even as Brethren, and not as enemies, neither avoyding therfore one anothers company, much lesse defaming one another. Now as the Parson is in Law, so is he in sicknesse also: if there be any of his flock sick, hee is their Physician, or at least his Wife, of whom in stead of the qualities of the world, he asks no other, but to have the skill of healing a wound, or helping the sick. But if neither himselfe, nor his wife have the skil, and his means serve, hee keepes some young practitioner in his house for the benefit of his Parish, whom yet he ever exhorts not to exceed his bounds, but in tickle cases to call in help. If all fail, then he keeps good correspondence with some neighbour Phisician, and entertaines him for the Cure of his Parish. Yet is it easie for any Scholer to attaine to such a measure of Phisick, as may be of much use to him both for himself, and others. This is done by seeing one Anatomy,[1] reading one Book of Phisick, having one Herball by him. And let *Fernelius* be the Phisick Authour, for he writes briefly, neatly, and judiciously; especially let his Method of Phisick be diligently perused, as being the practicall part, and of most use. Now both the reading of him, and the knowing of

[1] a skeleton, or dissected body.

THE COUNTRY PARSON

herbs may be done at such times, as they may be an
help, and a recreation to more divine studies, Nature
serving Grace both in comfort of diversion, and the
benefit of application when need requires; as also by
way of illustration, even as our Saviour made plants
and seeds to teach the people: for he was the true
householder, who bringeth out of his treasure things
new and old; the old things of Philosophy, and the new
of Grace; and maketh the one serve the other. And I
conceive, our Saviour did this for three reasons: first,
that by familiar things hee might make his Doctrine
slip the more easily into the hearts even of the meanest.
Secondly, that labouring people (whom he chiefly con-
sidered) might have every where monuments of his
Doctrine, remembring in gardens, his mustard-seed, and
lillyes; in the field, his seed-corn, and tares; and so not be
drowned altogether in the works of their vocation, but
sometimes lift up their minds to better things, even in
the midst of their pains. Thirdly, that he might set a
Copy for Parsons. In the knowledge of simples, wherein
the manifold wisedome of God is wonderfully to be
seen, one thing would be carefully observed; which is,
to know what herbs may be used in stead of drugs of
the same nature, and to make the garden the shop: For
home-bred medicines are both more easie for the
Parsons purse, and more familiar for all mens bodyes.
So, where the Apothecary useth either for loosing,
Rubarb, or for binding, Bolearmena, the Parson useth
damask or white Roses for the one, and plantaine,
shepherds purse, knot-grasse for the other, and that with
better successe. As for spices, he doth not onely prefer
home-bred things before them, but condemns them for

[53]

vanities, and so shuts them out of his family, esteeming
that there is no spice comparable, for herbs, to rose-
mary, time, savoury, mints; and for seeds, to Fennell,
and Carroway seeds. Accordingly, for salves, his wife
seeks not the city, but preferrs her garden and fields
before all outlandish gums. And surely hyssope,
valerian, mercury, adders tongue, yerrow, melilot, and
Saint *Johns* wort made into a salve; And Elder, camomill,
mallowes, comphrey and smallage made into a Poultis,
have done great and rare cures. In curing of any, the
Parson and his Family use to premise prayers, for this
is to cure like a Parson, and this raiseth the action from
the Shop, to the Church. But though the Parson sets
forward all Charitable deeds, yet he looks not in this
point of Curing beyond his own Parish, except the
person bee so poor, that he is not able to reward the
Phisician : for as hee is Charitable, so he is just also.
Now it is a justice and debt to the Common-wealth he
lives in, not to incroach on others Professions, but to
live on his own. And justice is the ground of Charity.

CHAPTER XXIV

The Parson arguing

The Countrey Parson, if there be any of his parish
that hold strange Doctrins, useth all possible diligence
to reduce them to the common Faith. The first means
he useth is Prayer, beseeching the Father of lights to
open their eyes, and to give him power so to fit his

discourse to them, that it may effectually pierce their hearts, and convert them. The second means is a very loving, and sweet usage of them, both in going to, and sending for them often, and in finding out Courtesies to place on them; as in their tithes, or otherwise. The third means is the observation what is the main foundation, and pillar of their cause, whereon they rely; as if he be a Papist, the Church is the hinge he turnes on; if a Schismatick, scandall.[1] Wherefore the Parson hath diligently examined these two with himselfe, as what the Church is, how it began, how it proceeded, whether it be a rule to it selfe, whether it hath a rule, whether having a rule, it ought not to be guided by it; whether any rule in the world be obscure, and how then should the best be so, at least in fundamentall things, the obscurity in some points being the exercise of the Church, the light in the foundations being the guide; The Church needing both an evidence, and an exercise. So for Scandall : what scandall is, when given or taken; whether, there being two precepts, one of obeying Authority, the other of not giving scandall, that ought not to be preferred, especially since in disobeying there is scandall also : whether things once indifferent, being made by the precept of Authority more than indifferent, it be in our power to omit or refuse them. These and the like points hee hath accurately digested, having ever besides two great helps and powerfull perswaders on his side; the one, a strict religious life; the other an humble, and ingenuous search of truth; being unmoved in arguing, and voyd of all contentiousnesse : which are two great lights able to dazle the eyes of the mis-led,

[1] 'stumbling block'.

while they consider, that God cannot be wanting to them in Doctrine, to whom he is so gracious in Life.

CHAPTER XXV

The Parson punishing

Whensoever the Countrey Parson proceeds so farre as to call in Authority, and to do such things of legall opposition either in the presenting, or punishing of any, as the vulgar ever consters for signes of ill will; he forbears not in any wise to use the delinquent as before, in his behaviour and carriage towards him, not avoyding his company, or doing any thing of aversenesse, save in the very act of punishment: neither doth he esteem him for an enemy, but as a brother still, except some small and temporary estranging may corroborate the punishment to a better subduing, and humbling of the delinquent; which if it happily take effect, he then comes on the faster, and makes so much the more of him, as before he alienated himselfe; doubling his regards, and shewing by all means, that the delinquents returne is to his advantage.

CHAPTER XXVI

The Parson's eye

The Countrey Parson at spare times from action, standing on a hill, and considering his Flock, discovers two sorts of vices, and two sorts of vicious persons. There are some vices, whose natures are always cleer, and evident, as Adultery, Murder, Hatred, Lying, &c. There are other vices, whose natures, at least in the beginning, are dark and obscure: as Covetousnesse, and Gluttony. So likewise there are some persons, who abstain not even from known sins; there are others, who when they know a sin evidently, they commit it not. It is true indeed, they are long a knowing it, being partiall to themselves, and witty to others who shall reprove them from it. A man may be both Covetous, and Intemperate, and yet hear Sermons against both, and himselfe condemn both in good earnest: and the reason hereof is, because the nature of these vices being not evidently discussed, or known commonly, the beginnings of them are not easily observable: and the beginnings of them are not observed, because of the suddain passing from that which was just now lawfull, to that which is presently unlawfull, even in one continued action. So a man dining, eats at first lawfully; but proceeding on, comes to do unlawfully, even before he is aware; not knowing the bounds of the action, nor when his eating begins to be unlawfull. So a man storing

up mony for his necessary provisions, both in present
for his family, and in future for his children, hardly per-
ceives when his storing becomes unlawfull : yet is there
a period for his storing, and a point, or center, when his
storing, which was even now good, passeth from good
to bad. Wherefore the Parson being true to his businesse,
hath exactly sifted the definitions of all vertues, and
vices; especially canvasing those, whose natures are
most stealing, and beginnings uncertaine. Particularly,
concerning these two vices, not because they are all that
are of this dark, and creeping disposition, but for
example sake, and because they are most common, he
thus thinks : first, for covetousnes, he lays this ground :
Whosoever when a just occasion cals, either spends not
at all, or not in some proportion to Gods blessing upon
him, is covetous. The reason of the ground is manifest,
because wealth is given to that end to supply our
occasions. Now, if I do not give every thing its end, I
abuse the Creature, I am false to my reason which
should guide me, I offend the supreme Judg, in pervert-
ing that order which he hath set both to things, and to
reason. The application of the ground would be
infinite; but in brief, a poor man is an occasion, my
countrey is an occasion, my friend is an occasion,
my Table is an occasion, my apparell is an occasion :
if in all these, and those more which concerne
me, I either do nothing, or pinch, and scrape, and
squeeze blood undecently to the station wherein God
hath placed me, I am Covetous. More particularly,
and to give one instance for all, if God have
given me servants, and I either provide too little for
them, or that which is unwholsome, being sometimes

[58]

baned meat, sometimes too salt, and so not competent nourishment, I am Covetous. I bring this example, because men usually think, that servants for their mony are as other things that they buy, even as a piece of wood, which they may cut, or hack, or throw into the fire, and so they pay them their wages, all is well. Nay, to descend yet more particularly, if a man hath where-withall to buy a spade, and yet hee chuseth rather to use his neighbours, and wear out that, he is covetous. Nevertheless, few bring covetousness thus low, or con-sider it so narrowly, which yet ought to be done, since there is a Justice in the least things, and for the least there shall be a judgment. Country people are full of these petty injustices, being cunning to make use of another, and spare themselves : and Scholers ought to be diligent in the observation of these, and driving of their generall Schoole rules ever to the smallest actions of Life; which while they dwell in their bookes, they will never finde; but being seated in the Countrey, and doing their duty faithfully, they will soon discover : especially if they carry their eyes ever open, and fix them on their charge, and not on their preferment. Secondly, for Gluttony, The Parson lays this ground : He that either for quantity eats more then his health or imployments will bear, or for quality is licorous after dainties, is a glutton; as he that eats more then his estate will bear, is a Prodigall; and hee that eats offensively to the Com-pany, either in his order, or length of eating, is scan-dalous and uncharitable. These three rules generally comprehend the faults of eating, and the truth of them needs no proofe : so that men must eat neither to the disturbance of their health, nor of their affairs, (which being overburdened, or studying dainties too much, they cannot wel dispatch) nor of their estate, nor of their brethren. One act in these things is bad, but it is the custome and habit that names a glutton. Many think they are at more liberty then they are, as if they were Masters of their health, and so they will stand to the pain, all is well. But to eat to ones hurt, comprehends, besides the hurt, an act against reason, because it is un-naturall to hurt ones self; and this they are not masters of. Yet of hurtfull things, I am more bound to abstain from those, which by mine own experience I have found hurtfull, then from those which by a Common tradition, and vulgar knowledge are reputed to be so. That which is said of hurtfull meats, extends to hurtfull drinks also. As for the quantity, touching our imploy-ments, none must eat so as to disable themselves from a fit discharging either of Divine duties, or duties of their calling. So that if after dinner they are not fit (or un-weeldy) either to pray, or work, they are gluttons. Not that all must presently work after dinner; (For they rather must not work, especially Students, and those that are weakly,) but that they must rise so, as that it is not meate or drinke that hinders them from working. To guide them in this, there are three rules : first, the custome, and knowledg of their own body, and what it can well disgest : The second, the feeling of them-selves in time of eating, which because it is deceitfull; (for one thinks in eating, that he can eat more, then afterwards he finds true :) The third is the observation with what appetite they sit down. This last rule joyned with the first, never fails. For knowing what one usually can well digest, and feeling when I go to meat in what disposition I am, either hungry or not, according as I feele my self, either I take my wonted proportion, or diminish of it. Yet Phisicians bid those that would live in health, not keep an uniform diet, but to feed variously, now more, now lesse: And *Gerson*, a spirituall man, wisheth all to incline rather to too much, then to too little; his reason is, because diseases of exinanation are more dangerous, then diseases of repletion. But the Parson distinguisheth according to his double aime, either of Abstinence a morall vertue, or Mortification a divine. When he deals with any that is heavy, and carnall; he gives him those freer rules: but when he meets with a refined, and heavenly disposition, he carryes them higher, even somtimes to a forgetting of themselves, knowing that there is one, who when they forget, remembers for them; As when the people hungred and thirsted after our Saviours Doctrine, and tarryed so long at it, that they would have fainted, had they returned empty, He suffered it not; but rather made food miraculously, then suffered so good desires to miscarry.

CHAPTER XXVII

The Parson in mirth

The Countrey Parson is generally sad, because hee knows nothing but the Crosse of Christ, his minde being defixed on it with those nailes wherewith his Master was: or if he have any leisure to look off from thence, he meets continually with two most sad spectacles, Sin, and Misery; God dishonoured every day, and man afflicted. Neverthelesse, he somtimes refresheth himselfe, as knowing that nature will not bear everlasting droopings, and that pleasantnesse of disposition is a great key to do good; not onely because all men shun the company of perpetuall severity, but also for that when they are in company, instructions seasoned with pleasantnesse, both enter sooner, and roote deeper. Wherefore he condescends to humane frailties both in himselfe and others; and intermingles some mirth in his discourses occasionally, according to the pulse of the hearer.

CHAPTER XXVIII

The Parson in Contempt

The Countrey Parson knows well, that both for the generall ignominy which is cast upon the profession, and much more for those rules, which out of his choysest judgment hee hath resolved to observe, and which are described in this Book, he must be despised; because this hath been the portion of God his Master, and of Gods Saints his Brethren, and this is foretold, that it shall be so still, until things be no more. Neverthelesse, according to the Apostles rule, he endeavours that none shall despise him; especially in his own Parish he suffers it not to his utmost power; for that, where contempt is, there is no room for instruction. This he procures, first by his holy and unblameable life; which carries a reverence with it, even above contempt. Secondly, by a courteous carriage, & winning behaviour: he that wil be respected, must respect; doing kindnesses, but receiving none; at least of those, who are apt to despise: for this argues a height and eminency of mind, which is not easily despised, except it degenerate to pride. Thirdly, by a bold and impartial reproof, even of the best in the Parish, when occasion requires: for this may produce hatred in those that are reproved, but never contempt either in them, or others. Lastly, if the contempt shall proceed so far as to do any thing punishable by law, as contempt is apt to do, if it be not thwarted, *the Parson having a due respect both to the person, and to the cause, referreth the whole matter to the examination, and punishment of those which are in Authority*; that so the sentence lighting upon one, the example may reach to all. But if the Contempt be not punishable by Law, or being so, the Parson think it in his discretion either unfit, or bootelesse to contend, then when any despises him, he takes it either in an humble way, saying nothing at all; or else in a slighting way, shewing that reproaches touch him no more, then a stone thrown against heaven, where he is, and lives; or in a sad way, greived at his own, and others sins, which continually breake Gods Laws, and dishonour him with those mouths, which he continually fils, and feeds: or else in a doctrinall way, saying to the contemner, Alas, why do you thus? you hurt your selfe, not me; he that throws a stone at another, hits himselfe; and so between gentle reasoning, and pitying, he overcomes the evill: or lastly, in a Triumphant way, being glad, and joyfull, that hee is

[63]

made conformable to his Master; and being in the world as he was, hath this undoubted pledge of his salvation. These are the five shields, wherewith the Godly receive the darts of the wicked; leaving anger, and retorting, and revenge to the children of the world, whom anothers ill mastereth, and leadeth captive without any resistance, even in resistance, to the same destruction. For while they resist the person that reviles, they resist not the evill which takes hold of them, and is farr the worse enemy.

CHAPTER XXIX

The Parson with his Church-Wardens

The Countrey Parson doth often, both publickly, and privately instruct his Church-Wardens, what a great Charge lyes upon them, and that indeed the whole order and discipline of the Parish is put into their hands. If himselfe reforme any thing, it is out of the overflowing of his Conscience, whereas they are to do it by Command, and by Oath. Neither hath the place its dignity from the Ecclesiasticall Laws only, since even by the Common Statute-Law they are taken for a kinde of Corporation, as being persons enabled by that Name to take moveable goods, or chattels, and to sue, and to be sued at the Law concerning such goods for the use and profit of their Parish : and by the same Law they are to levy penalties for negligence in resorting to church, or for disorderly carriage in time of divine service. Wherefore the Parson suffers not the place to be vilified or debased, by being cast on to the lower ranke of people; but invites and urges the best into it, shewing that they do not loose, or go lesse, but gaine by it; it being the greatest honor of this world, to do God and his chosen service; or as *David* says, to be even a door-keeper in the house of God. Now the Canons being the Church-wardens rule, the Parson adviseth them to read, or hear them read often, as also the visitation Articles, which are grounded upon the Canons, that so they may know their duty, and keep their oath the better; in which regard, considering the great Consequence of their place, and more of their oath, he wisheth them by no means to spare any, though never so great; but if after gentle, and neighbourly admonitions they still persist in ill, to present them; yea though they be tenants, or otherwise ingaged to the delinquent : for their obligation to God, and to their own soul, is above any temporall tye. Do well, and right, and let the world sinke.

CHAPTER XXX

The Parson's Consideration of Providence

The Countrey Parson considering the great aptnesse Countrey people have to think that all things come by a kind of naturall course; and that if they sow and soyle[1] their grounds, they must have corn; if they keep and fodder well their cattel, they must have milk, and

[1] manure.

Calves; labours to reduce them to see Gods hand in all things, and to beleeve, that things are not set in such an inevitable order, but that God often changeth it according as he sees fit, either for reward or punishment. To this end he represents to his flock, that God hath and exerciseth a threefold power in every thing which concernes man. The first is a sustaining power; the second a governing power; the third a spirituall power. By his sustaining power he preserves and actuates every thing in his being; so that corne doth not grow by any other vertue, then by that which he continually supplyes, as the corn needs it; without which supply the corne would instantly dry up, as a river would if the fountain were stopped. And it is observable, that if anything could presume of an inevitable course, and constancy in its operations, certainly it should be either the sun in heaven, or the fire on earth, by reason of their fierce, strong, and violent natures: yet when God pleased, the sun stood stil, the fire burned not. By Gods governing power he preserves and orders the references of things one to the other, so that though the corn do grow, and be preserved in that act by his sustaining power, yet if he suite not other things to the growth, as seasons, and weather, and other accidents by his governing power, the fairest harvests come to nothing. And it is observeable, that God delights to have men feel, and acknowledg, and reverence his power, and therefore he often overturnes things, when they are thought past danger; that is his time of interposing: As when a Merchant hath a ship come home after many a storme, which it hath escaped, he destroyes it sometimes in the very Haven; or if the goods be housed, a fire hath broken forth, and suddenly consumed them. Now this he doth, that men should perpetuate, and not break off their acts of dependance, how faire soever the opportunities present themselves. So that if a farmer should depend upon God all the yeer, and being ready to put hand to sickle, shall then secure himself, and think all cock-sure; then God sends such weather, as lays the corn, and destroys it : or if he depend on God further, even till he imbarn his corn, and then think all sure; God sends a fire, and consumes all that he hath : For that he ought not to break off, but to continue his dependance on God, not onely before the corne is inned, but after also; and indeed, to depend, and fear continually. The third power is spirituall, by which God turnes all outward blessings to inward advantages. So that if a Farmer hath both a faire harvest, and that also well inned, and imbarned, and continuing safe there; yet if God give him not the Grace to use, and utter this well, all his advantages are to his losse. Better were his corne burnt, then not spiritually improved. And it is observable in this, how Gods goodnesse strives with mans refractorinesse; Man would sit down at this world, God bids him sell it, and purchase a better : Just as a Father, who hath in his hand an apple, and a piece of Gold under it; the Child comes, and with pulling, gets the apple out of his Fathers hand : his Father bids him throw it away, and he will give him the gold for it, which the Child utterly refusing, eats it, and is troubled with wormes : So is the carnall and wilfull man with the worm of the grave in this world, and the worm of Conscience in the next.

[67]

CHAPTER XXXI

The Parson in Liberty

The Countrey Parson observing the manifold wiles of
Satan (who playes his part sometimes in drawing Gods
Servants from him, sometimes in perplexing them in
the service of God) stands fast in the Liberty wherewith
Christ hath made us free. This Liberty he compasseth
by one distinction, and that is, of what is Necessary, and
what is Additionary. As for example: It is necessary
that all Christians should pray twice a day, every day
of the week, and four times on Sunday, if they be well.
This is so necessary, and essentiall to a Christian, that
he cannot without this maintain himself in a Christian
state. Besides this, the Godly have ever added some
houres of prayer, as at nine, or at three, or at midnight,
or as they think fit, & see cause, or rather as Gods
spirit leads them. But these prayers are not necessary,
but additionary. Now it so happens, that the godly
petitioner upon some emergent interruption in the day,
or by oversleeping himself at night, omits his additionary
prayer. Upon this his mind begins to be perplexed, and
troubled, and Satan, who knows the exigent, blows the
fire, endeavouring to disorder the Christian, and put him
out of his station, and to inlarge the perplexity, untill
it spread, and taint his other duties of piety, which none
can perform so wel in trouble, as in calmness. Here the
Parson interposeth with his distinction, and shews the

perplexed Christian, that this prayer being additionary, not necessary; taken in, not commanded, the omission thereof upon just occasion ought by no means to trouble him. God knows the occasion as wel as he, and He is as a gracious Father, who more accepts a common course of devotion, then dislikes an occasionall interruption. And of this he is so to assure himself, as to admit no scruple, but to go on as cheerfully, as if he had not been interrupted. By this it is evident, that the distinction is of singular use and comfort, especially to pious minds, which are ever tender, and delicate. But here there are two Cautions to be added. First, that this interruption proceed not out of slacknes, or coldness, which will appear if the Pious soul foresee and prevent such interruptions, what he may, before they come, and when for all that they do come, he be a little affected therewith, but not afflicted, or troubled; if he resent it to a mislike, but not a griefe. Secondly, that this interruption proceede not out of shame. As for example: A godly man, not out of superstition, but of reverence to Gods house, resolves whenever he enters into a Church, to kneel down, and pray, either blessing God, that he will be pleased to dwell among men; or beseeching him, that whenever he repaires to his house, he may behave himself so as befits so great a presence; and this briefly. But it happens, that neer the place where he is to pray, he spyes some scoffing ruffian, who is likely to deride him for his paines: if he now, shall either for fear or shame, break his custome, he shall do passing ill: so much the rather ought he to proceed, as that by this he may take into his Prayer humiliation also. On the other side, if I am to visit the sick in haste, and my neerest way ly through the Church, I will not doubt to go without staying to pray there (but onely, as I passe, in my heart) because this kinde of Prayer is additionary, not necessary, and the other duty overweighs it: So that if any scruple arise, I will throw it away, and be most confident, that God is not displeased. This distinction may runne through all Christian duties, and it is a great stay and setling to religious souls.

CHAPTER XXXII

The Parson's Surveys

The Countrey Parson hath not onely taken a particular Survey of the faults of his own Parish, but a generall also of the diseases of the time, that so, when his occasions carry him abroad, or bring strangers to him, he may be the better armed to encounter them. The great and nationall sin of this Land he esteems to be Idlenesse; great in it selfe, and great in Consequence: For when men have nothing to do, then they fall to drink, to steal, to whore, to scoffe, to revile, to all sorts of gamings. Come, say they, we have nothing to do, lets go to the Tavern, or to the stews, or what not. Wherefore the Parson strongly opposeth this sin, whersoever he goes. And because Idleness is twofold, the one in having no calling, the other in walking carelesly in our calling, he first represents to every body the necessity of a vocation. The reason of this assertion is taken from the nature of man, wherein God hath placed two great

Instruments, Reason in the soul, and a hand in the Body, as ingagements of working: So that even in Paradise man had a calling, and how much more out of Paradise, when the evills which he is now subject unto, may be prevented, or diverted by reasonable imployment. Besides, every gift or ability is a talent to be accounted for, and to be improved to our Masters Advantage. Yet is it also a debt to our Countrey to have a Calling, and it concernes the Common-wealth, that none should be idle, but all busied. Lastly, riches are the blessing of God, and the great Instrument of doing admirable good; therfore all are to procure them honestly, and seasonably, when they are not better imployed. Now this reason crosseth not our Saviours precept of selling what we have, because when we have sold all, and given it to the poor, we must not be idle, but labour to get more, that we may give more, according to St. *Pauls* rule, *Ephes.* 4.28. I *Thes.* 4.11,12. So that our Saviours selling is so far from crossing Saint *Pauls* working, that it rather establisheth it, since they that have nothing, are fittest to work. Now because the onely opposer to this Doctrine is the Gallant, who is witty enough to abuse both others, and himself, and who is ready to ask, if he shall mend shoos, or what he shall do? Therfore the Parson unmoved, sheweth, that *ingenuous and fit* imployment is never wanting to those that seek it. But if it should be, the Assertion stands thus: All are either to have a Calling, or prepare for it: He that hath or can have yet no imployment, if he truly, and seriously prepare for it, he is safe and within bounds. Wherefore all are either presently to enter into a Calling, if they be fit for it, and it for them; or else to examine with

care, and advice, what they are fittest for, and to pre-
pare for that with all diligence. But it will not be amisse
in this exceeding usefull point to descend to particulars :
for exactnesse lyes in particulars. Men are either single,
or marryed: The marryed and house-keeper hath his
hands full, if he do what he ought to do. For there are
two branches of his affaires; first, the improvement of
his family, by bringing them up in the fear and nurture
of the Lord; and secondly, the improvement of his
grounds, by drowning, or draining, or stocking, or
fencing, and ordering his land to the best advantage
both of himself, and his neighbours. The *Italian* says,
None fouls his hands in his own businesse : and it is an
honest, and just care, so it exceed not bounds, for every
one to imploy himselfe to the advancement of his affairs,
that hee may have wherewithall to do good. But his
family is his best care, to labour Christian soules, and
raise them to their height, even to heaven; to dresse and
prune them, and take as much joy in a straight-growing
childe, or servant, as a Gardiner doth in a choice tree.
Could men finde out this delight, they would seldome
be from home; whereas now, of any place, they are least
there. But if after all this care well dispatched, the
house-keepers Family be so small, and his dexterity so
great, that he have leisure to look out, the Village or
Parish which either he lives in, or is neer unto it, is his
imployment. Hee considers every one there, and either
helps them in particular, or hath generall Propositions
to the whole Towne or Hamlet, of advancing the pub-
lick Stock, and managing Commons, or Woods, accord-
ing as the place suggests. But if hee may bee of the
Commission of Peace, there is nothing to that: No

Common-wealth in the world hath a braver Institution then that of Justices of the Peace: For it is both a security to the King, who hath so many dispersed Officers at his beck throughout the Kingdome, accountable for the publick good; and also an honourable Imployment of a Gentle, or Noble-man in the Country he lives in, inabling him with power to do good, and to restrain all those, who else might both trouble him and the whole State. Wherefore it behoves all, who are come to the gravitie, and ripenesse of judgement for so excellent a Place, not to refuse, but rather to procure it. And whereas there are usually three Objections made against the Place; the one, the abuse of it, by taking petty Countrey bribes; the other, the casting of it on mean persons, especially in some Shires: and lastly, the trouble of it: These are so far from deterring any good man from the place, that they kindle them rather to redeem the Dignity either from true faults, or unjust aspersions. Now, for single men, they are either Heirs, or younger Brothers: The Heirs are to prepare in all the fore-mentioned points against the time of their practice. Therefore they are to mark their Fathers discretion in ordering his House and Affairs; and also elsewhere, when they see any remarkable point of Education or good husbandry, and to transplant it in time to his own home, with the same care as others, when they meet with good fruit, get a graffe of the tree, inriching their Orchard, and neglecting their House. Besides, they are to read Books of Law, and Justice; especially, the Statutes at large. As for better Books of Divinity, they are not in this Consideration, because we are about a Calling, and a preparation thereunto. But chiefly, and above all things, they are to frequent Sessions and Sizes; for it is both an honor which they owe to the Reverend Judges and Magistrates, to attend them, at least in their Shire; and it is a great advantage to know the practice of the Land; for our Law is Practice. Sometimes he may go to Court, as the eminent place both of good and ill. At other times he is to travell over the King's Dominions, cutting out the Kingdome into Portions, which every yeer he surveys peece-meal. When there is a Parliament, he is to endeavour by all means to be a Knight or Burgess there; for there is no School to a Parliament. And when he is there, he must not only be a morning man, but at Committees also; for there the particulars are exactly discussed, which are brought from thence to the House but in generall. When none of these occasions call him abroad, every morning that hee is at home hee must either ride the Great Horse, or exercise some of his Military gestures. For all Gentlemen, that are now weakned, and disarmed with sedentary lives, are to know the use of their Arms : and as the Husbandman labours for them, so must they fight for, and defend them, when occasion calls. This is the duty of each to other, which they ought to fulfill : And the Parson is a lover of and exciter to justice in all things, even as *John the Baptist* squared out to every one (even to Souldiers) what to do. As for younger Brothers, those whom the Parson finds loose, and not ingaged into some Profession by their Parents, whose neglect in this point is intolerable, and a shamefull wrong both to the Common-wealth, and their own House : To them, after he hath shew'd the unlawfulness of spending the day in dressing, Complementing, visiting, and sporting, he first commends the study of the Civill Law, as a brave, and wise knowledg, the Professours whereof were much imployed by Queen *Elizabeth*, because it is the key of Commerce, and discovers the Rules of forraine Nations. Secondly, he commends the Mathematicks, as the only wonder-working knowledg, and therefore requiring the best spirits. After the severall knowledg of these, he adviseth to insist and dwell chiefly on the two noble branches therof, of Fortification, and Navigation; The one being usefull to all Countreys, and the other especially to Ilands. But if the young Gallant think these Courses dull, and phlegmatick, where can he busie himself better, then in those new Plantations, and discoveryes, which are not only a noble, but also as they may be handled, a religious imployment? Or let him travel into *Germany*, and *France*, and observing the Artifices, and Manufactures there, transplant them hither, as divers have done lately, to our Countrey's advantage.

CHAPTER XXXIII

The Parson's Library[1]

The Countrey Parson's Library is a holy Life: for besides the blessing that that brings upon it, there being

[1] This curiously named chapter might suggest that Herbert disapproved of books and reading. That this was far from being the case is made clear elsewhere in *The Country Parson* as well as in his other writings and his own practice.

a promise, that if the Kingdome of God be first sought, all other things shall be added, even it selfe is a Sermon. For the temptations with which a good man is beset, and the ways which he used to overcome them, being told to another, whether in private conference, or in the Church, are a Sermon. Hee that hath considered how to carry himself at table about his appetite, if he tell this to another, preacheth; and much more feelingly, and judiciously, then he writes his rules of temperance out of bookes. So that the Parson having studied, and mastered all his lusts and affections within, and the whole Army of Temptations without, hath ever so many sermons ready penn'd, as he hath victories. And it fares in this as it doth in Physick: He that hath been sick of a Consumption, and knows what recovered him, is a Physitian so far as he meetes with the same disease, and temper; and can much better, and particularly do it, then he that is generally learned, and was never sick. And if the same person had been sick of all diseases, and were recovered of all by things that he knew; there were no such Physician as he, both for skill and tendernesse. Just so it is in Divinity, and that not without manifest reason: for though the temptations may be diverse in divers Christians, yet the victory is alike in all, being by the self-same Spirit. Neither is this true onely in the military state of a Christian life, but even in the peaceable also; when the servant of God, freed for a while from temptation, in a quiet sweetnesse seeks how to please his God. Thus the Parson considering that repentance is the great vertue of the Gospel, and one of the first steps of pleasing God, having for his owne use examined the nature of it, is able to explaine it after to others. And particularly, having doubted sometimes, whether his repentance were true, or at least in that degree it ought to be, since he found himselfe sometimes to weepe more for the losse of some temporall things, then for offending God, he came at length to this resolution, that repentance is an act of the mind, not of the Body, even as the Originall signifies; and that the chiefe thing, which God in Scriptures requires, is the heart, and the spirit, and to worship him in truth, and spirit. Wherefore in case a Christian endeavour to weep, and cannot, since we are not Masters of our bodies, this sufficeth. And consequently he found, that the essence of repentance, that it may be alike in all Gods children (which as concerning weeping it cannot be, some being of a more melting temper then others) consisteth in a true detestation of the soul, abhorring, and renouncing sin, and turning unto God in truth of heart, and newnesse of life : Which acts of repentance are and must be found in all Gods servants : Not that weeping is not usefull, where it can be, that so the body may joyn in the grief, as it did in the sin; but that, so the other acts be, that is not necessary : so that he as truly repents, who performes the other acts of repentance, when he cannot more, as he that weeps a floud of tears. This Instruction and comfort the Parson getting for himself, when he tels it to others, becomes a Sermon. The like he doth in other Christian vertues, as of Faith, and Love, and the Cases of Conscience belonging thereto, wherein (as Saint *Paul* implyes that he ought, *Romans* 2) hee first preacheth to himselfe, and then to others.

CHAPTER XXXIV

The Parson's Dexterity in applying of Remedies

The Countrey Parson knows, that there is a double
state of a Christian even in this Life, the one military,
the other peaceable. The military is, when we are
assaulted with temptations either from within or from
without. The Peaceable is, when the Divell for a time
leaves us, as he did our Saviour, and the Angels minister
to us their owne food, even joy, and peace; and comfort
in the holy Ghost. These two states were in our Saviour,
not only in the beginning of his preaching, but after-
wards also, as *Mat.* 22.35. He was tempted: And *Luke*
10.21. He rejoyced in Spirit: And they must be likewise
in all that are his. Now the Parson having a Spirituall
Judgement, according as he discovers any of his Flock
to be in one or the other state, so he applies himselfe to
them. Those that he findes in the peaceable state, he
adviseth to be very vigilant, and not to let go the raines
as soon as the horse goes easie. Particularly, he coun-
selleth them to two things: First, to take heed, lest
their quiet betray them (as it is apt to do) to a coldnesse,
and a carelesnesse in their devotions, but to labour still
to be as fervent in Christian Duties, as they remember
themselves were, when affliction did blow the Coals.
Secondly, not to take the full compasse, and liberty of
their Peace: not to eate of all those dishes at table,
which even their present health otherwise admits; nor

to store their house with all those furnitures which even their present plenty of wealth otherwise admits; nor when they are among them that are merry, to extend themselves to all that mirth, which the present occasion of wit and company otherwise admits; but to put bounds, and hoopes to their joyes: so will they last the longer, and when they depart, returne the sooner. If we would judg ourselves, we should not be judged; and if we would bound our selves, we should not be bounded. But if they shall fear, that at such, or such a time their peace and mirth have carryed them further then this moderation, then to take *Jobs* admirable Course, who sacrificed lest his Children should have transgressed in their mirth: So let them go, and find some poore afflicted soul, and there be bountifull, and liberall; for with such sacrifices God is well pleased. Those that the Parson findes in the military state, he fortifyes, and strengthens with his utmost skill. Now in those that are tempted, whatsoever is unruly, falls upon two heads; either they think, that there is none that can or will look after things, but all goes by chance, or wit: Or else, though there be a great Governour of all things, yet to them he is lost, as if they said, God doth forsake and persecute them, and there is none to deliver them. If the Parson suspect the first, and find sparkes of such thoughts now and then to break forth, then without opposing directly (for disputation is no Cure for Atheisme) he scatters in his discourse three sorts of arguments; the first taken from Nature, the second from the Law, the third from Grace.

For Nature, he sees not how a house could be either built without a builder, or kept in repaire without a house-keeper. He conceives not possibly, how the windes should blow so much as they can, and the sea rage so much as it can, and all things do what they can, and all, not only without dissolution of the whole, but also of any part, by taking away so much as the usuall seasons of summer and winter, earing and harvest. Let the weather be what it will, still we have bread, though sometimes more, sometimes lesse; wherewith also a carefull *Joseph* might meet. He conceives not possibly, how he that would beleeve a Divinity, if he had been at the Creation of all things, should lesse beleeve it, seeing the Preservation of all things; For Preservation is a Creation; and more, it is a continued Creation, and a creation every moment.

Secondly, for the Law, there may be so evident, though unused a proof of Divinity taken from thence, that the Atheist, or Epicurian can have nothing to contradict. The Jewes yet live, and are known: they have their Law and Language bearing witnesse to them, and they to it: they are Circumcised to this day, and expect the promises of the Scripture; their Countrey also is known, the places, and rivers travelled unto, and frequented by others, but to them an unpenetrable rock, an unaccessible desert. Wherefore if the Jewes live, all the great wonders of old live in them, and then who can deny the stretched out arme of a mighty God? especially since it may be a just doubt, whether, considering the stubbornnesse of the Nation, their living then in their Countrey under so many miracles were a stranger thing, then their present exile, and disability to live in their Countrey. And it is observable, that this very thing was intended by God, that the Jewes should be his proof, and witnesses, as he calls them, *Isaiah* 43.12. And their very dispersion in all Lands, was intended not only for a punishment to them; but for an exciting of others by their sight, to the acknowledging of God, and his power, *Psalm* 59.11. And therefore this kind of Punishment was chosen rather then any other.

Thirdly, for Grace. Besides the continuall succession (since the Gospell) of holy men, who have born witness to the truth (there being no reason, why any should distrust Saint *Luke*, or *Tertullian*, or *Chrysostome*, more then *Tully*, *Virgill*, or *Livy*;) There are two Prophesies in the Gospel, which evidently argue Christs Divinity by their success: the one concerning the woman that spent the oyntment on our Saviour, for which he told, that it should never be forgotten, but with the Gospel it selfe be preached to all ages, *Matth.* 26.13. The other concerning the destruction of *Jerusalem*; of which our Saviour said, that that generation should not passe, till all were fulfilled, *Luke* 21.32. Which *Josephus's* History confirmeth, and the continuance of which verdict is yet evident. To these might be added the Preaching of the Gospel in all Nations, *Matthew* 24.14. which we see even miraculously effected in these new discoveryes, God turning mens Covetousnesse, and Ambitions to the effecting of his word. Now a prophesie is a wonder sent to Posterity, least they complaine of want of wonders. It is a letter sealed, and sent, which to the bearer is but paper, but to the receiver, and opener, is full of power. Hee that saw Christ open a blind mans eyes, saw not more Divinity, then he that reads the woman's oyntment in the Gospell, or sees

[81]

Jerusalem destroyed. With some of these heads enlarged, and woven into his discourse, at severall times and occasions, the Parson setleth wavering minds. But if he sees them neerer desperation, then Atheisme; not so much doubting a God, as that he is theirs; then he dives unto the boundlesse Ocean of Gods Love, and the unspeakeable riches of his loving kindnesse. He hath one argument unanswerable. If God hate them, either he doth it as they are Creatures, dust and ashes; or as they are sinfull. As Creatures, he must needs love them; for no perfect Artist ever yet hated his owne worke. As sinfull, he must much more love them; because notwithstanding his infinite hate of sinne, his Love overcame that hate; and with an exceeding great victory, which in the Creation needed not, gave them love for love, even the son of his love out of his bosome of love. So that man, which way soever he turnes, hath two pledges of Gods Love, that in the mouth of two or three witnesses every word may be established; the one in his being, the other in his sinfull being: and this as the more faulty in him, so the more glorious in God. And all may certainly conclude, that God loves them, till either they despise that Love, or despaire of his Mercy : not any sin else, but is within his Love; but the despising of Love must needs be without it. The thrusting away of his arme makes us onely not embraced.

CHAPTER XXXV

The Parson's Condescending

The Countrey Parson is a Lover of old Customes, if
they be good, and harmlesse; and the rather, because
Countrey People are much addicted to them, so that to
favour them therein is to win their hearts, and to oppose
them therin is to deject them. If there be any ill in
the custome, that may be severed from the good, he
pares the apple, and gives them the clean to feed on.
Particularly, he loves Procession, and maintains it,
because there are contained therein 4 manifest advan-
tages. First, a blessing of God for the fruits of the field:
Secondly, justice in the Preservation of bounds: Thirdly,
Charity in loving walking, and neighbourly accompany-
ing one another, with reconciling of differences at that
time, if there be any: Fourthly, Mercy in releeving the
poor by a liberall distribution and largesse, which at
that time is, or ought to be used. Wherefore he exacts
of all to bee present at the perambulation, and those
that withdraw, and sever themselves from it, he mis-
likes, and reproves as uncharitable, and unneighbourly;
and if they will not reforme, presents them. Nay, he is
so farre from condemning such assemblies, that he
rather procures them to be often, as knowing that
absence breedes strangeness, but presence love. Now
Love is his business, and aime; wherefore he likes well,
that his Parish at good times invite one another to their

houses, and he urgeth them to it: and sometimes, where he knowes there hath been or is a little difference, hee takes one of the parties, and goes with him to the other, and all dine or sup together. There is much preaching in this friendliness. Another old Custome there is of saying, when light is brought in, God send us the light of heaven; And the Parson likes this very well; neither is he affraid of praising, or praying to God at all times, but is rather glad of catching opportunities to do them. Light is a great Blessing, and as great as food, for which we give thanks: and those that thinke this superstitious, neither know superstition, nor themselves. As for those that are ashamed to use this forme, as being old, and obsolete, and not the fashion, he reformes, and teaches them, that at Baptisme they professed not to be ashamed of Christs Cross, or for any shame to leave that which is good. He that is ashamed in small things, will extend his pusillanimity to greater. Rather should a Christian Souldier take such occasions to harden himselfe, and to further his exercises of Mortification.

CHAPTER XXXVI

The Parson Blessing

The Countrey Parson wonders, that Blessing the people is in so little use with his brethren: whereas he thinks it not onely a grave, and reverend thing, but a beneficiall also. Those who use it not, do so either out of niceness, because they like the salutations, and complements, and formes of worldly language better; which conformity and fashionableness is so exceeding unbefitting a Minister, that it deserves reproof, not refutation: Or else, because they think it empty and superfluous. But that which the Apostles used so diligently in their writings, nay, which our Saviour himselfe used, *Marke* 10.16, cannot bee vain and superfluous. But this was not proper to Christ, or the Apostles only, no more then to be a spirituall Father was appropriated to them. And if temporall Fathers blesse their children, how much more may, and ought Spirituall Fathers? Besides, the Priests of the Old Testament were commanded to Blesse the people, and the forme thereof is prescribed, *Numb.* 6. Now as the Apostle argues in another case; if the Ministration of condemnation did bless, how shall not the ministration of the spirit exceed in blessing? The fruit of this blessing good *Hannah* found, and received with great joy, I *Sam.* 1.18, though it came from a man disallowed by God: for it was not the person, but Priesthood, that blessed; so that even ill Priests may blesse. Neither have the Ministers power of Blessing only, but also of cursing. So in the Old Testament *Elisha* cursed the children, 2 *Kin.* 2.24. which though our Saviour reproved as unfitting for his particular, who was to shew all humility before his Passion, yet he allows in his Apostles. And therfore St. *Peter* used that fearfull imprecation to *Simon Magus*, *Act.* 8. *Thy mony perish with thee*: and the event confirmed it. So did St. *Paul*, 2 *Tim.* 4.14. and 1 *Tim.* 1.20. Speaking of *Alexander* the Coppersmith, who had withstood his preaching, *The Lord* (saith he) *reward him according to his works.* And again, of *Hymeneus* and *Alexander*, he saith, he had *delivered them to Satan, that they might learn not to Blaspheme*. The formes both of Blessing, & cursing are expounded in the Common-Prayer-book: the one in, The Grace of our Lord Jesus Christ, &c. and: The Peace of God, &c. The other in generall, in the Commination. Now blessing differs from prayer, in assurance, because it is not performed by way of request, but of confidence, and power, effectually applying Gods favour to the blessed, by the interesting of that dignity wherewith God hath invested the Priest, and ingaging of Gods own power and institution for a blessing. The neglect of this duty in Ministers themselves, hath made the people also neglect it; so that they are so far from craving this benefit from their ghostly Father, that they oftentimes goe out of church, before he hath blessed them. In the time of Popery, the Priests *Benedicite*, and his holy water were over highly valued; and now we are fallen to the clean contrary, even from superstition to coldnes, and Atheism. But the Parson first values the gift in himself, and then teacheth his parish to value it. And it is observable, that if a Minister talke with a great man in the ordinary course of complementing language, he shall be esteemed as ordinary complementers; but if he often interpose a Blessing, when the other gives him just opportunity, by speaking any good, this unusuall form begets a reverence, and makes him esteemed according to his Profession. The same is to be observed in writing Letters also. To conclude, if all men are to blesse upon occasion, as appears *Rom.* 12.14. how much more those, who are spiritual Fathers?

CHAPTER XXXVII

Concerning detraction

The Countrey Parson perceiving, that most, when they are at leasure, make others faults their entertainment and discourse, and that even some good men think, so they speak truth, they may disclose anothers fault, finds it somwhat difficult how to proceed in this point. For if he absolutely shut up mens mouths, and forbid all disclosing of faults, many an evill may not only be, but also spread in his Parish, without any remedy (which cannot be applyed without notice) to the dishonor of God, and the infection of his flock, and the discomfort, discredit, & hinderance of the Pastor. On the other side, if it be unlawful to open faults, no benefit or advantage can make it lawfull : for we must not do evill, that good may come of it. Now the Parson taking this point to task, which is so exceeding useful, and hath taken so deep roote, that it seems the very life and substance of Conversation, hath proceeded thus far in the discussing of it. Faults are either notorious, or private. Again notorious faults are either such as are made known by common fame (and of these, those that know them, may talk, so they do it not with sport, but commiseration;) or else such as have passed judgment, & been corrected either by whipping, or imprisoning, or the like. Of these also men may talk, and more, they may discover them to those that know them not: because infamy is a part of the sentence against malefactours, which the Law intends, as is evident by those, which are branded for rogues, that they may be known; or put into the stocks, that they may be looked upon. But some may say, though the Law allow this, the Gospel doth not, which hath so much advanced Charity, and ranked backbiters among the generation of the wicked, *Rom.* 1.30. But this is easily answered: As the executioner is not uncharitable, that takes away the life of the condemned, except besides his office, he add a tincture of private malice in the joy, and hast of acting his part; so neither is he that defames him, whom the Law would have defamed, except he also do it out of rancour. For in infamy, all are executioners, and the Law gives a malefactour to all to be defamed. And as malefactors may lose & forfeit their goods, or life; so may they their good name, and the possession thereof, which before their offence and Judgment they had in all mens brests: for all are honest, till the contrary be proved. Besides, it concerns the Common-Wealth, that Rogues should be known, and Charity to the publick hath the precedence of private charity. So that it is so far from being a fault to discover such offenders, that it is a duty rather, which may do much good, and save much harme. Neverthelesse, if the punished delinquent shall be much troubled for his sins, and turne quite another man, doubtlesse then also mens affections and words must turne, and forbear to speak of that, which even God himself hath forgotten.

SELECTED POEMS

LOVE

LOVE

Love bade me welcome: yet my soul drew back,
      Guiltie of dust and sinne,
But quick-ey'd Love, observing me grow slack
      From my first entrance in,
Drew nearer to me, sweetly questioning,
      If I lack'd any thing.

A guest, I answer'd, worthy to be here:
      Love said, You shall be he.
I the unkinde, ungratefull? Ah my deare,
      I cannot look on thee.
Love took my hand, and smiling did reply,
      Who made the eyes but I?

Truth Lord, but I have marr'd them: let my shame
      Go where it doth deserve.
And know you not, sayes Love, who bore the blame?
      My deare, then I will serve.
You must sit down, sayes Love, and taste my meat:
      So I did sit and eat.[1]

---

[1] Blessed are those servants, whom the Lord when he cometh shall find watching: verily I say unto you, that he shall gird himself, and make them sit down to meat, and will come forth and serve them.

St Luke 12, 37

THE PILGRIMAGE[1]

I travell'd on, seeing the hill, where lay
        My expectation.
        A long it was and weary way.
        The gloomy cave of Desperation
I left on th' one, and on the other side
        The rock of Pride.

And so I came to Phansies medow strow'd
        With many a flower:
        Fair would I here have made abode,
        But I was quicken'd by my houre,
So to Cares cops I came, and there got through
        With much ado.

That led me to the wilde of Passion, which
        Some call the wold;
        A wasted place, but sometimes rich,
        Here I was robb'd of all my gold,
Save one good Angell[2] which a friend had ti'd
        Close to my side.

[1] A poem in which George Herbert's allegorical use of the countryside would seem to anticipate John Bunyan's *The Pilgrim's Progress* (1678).

[2] An Old English coin engraved with the Archangel Michael and the Dragon. Also the pilgrim's guardian angel.

At length I got unto the gladsome hill,
        Where lay my hope,
           Where lay my heart; and climbing still,
           When I had gain'd the brow and top,
A lake of brackish waters on the ground
        Was all I found.

With that abash'd and struck with many a sting
        Of swarming fears,
           I fell, and cry'd, Alas my King;
           Can both the way and end be tears?
Yet taking heart I rose, and then perceiv'd
        I was deceiv'd:

My hill was further: so I flung away,
        Yet heard a crie
           Just as I went, *None goes that way*
           And lives: If that be all, said I,
After so foul a journey death is fair,
        And but a chair.

THE QUIP[1]

The merrie world did on a day
With his train-bands and mates agree
To meet together, where I lay,
And all in sport to geere at me.

First, Beautie crept into a rose,
Which when I pluckt not, Sir, said she,
Tell me, I pray, Whose hands are those?
But thou shalt answer, Lord, for me.

Then Money came, and chinking still,
What tune is this, poore man? said he:
I heard in Musick you had skill.
But thou shalt answer, Lord, for me.

Then came brave Glorie puffing by
In silks that whistled, who but he?
He scarce allow'd me half an eie.
But thou shalt answer, Lord, for me.

Then came quick Wit and Conversation,
And he would needs a comfort be,
And, to be short, make an oration.
But thou shalt answer, Lord, for me.

Yet when the houre of thy designe
To answer these fine things shall come;
Speak not at large, say, I am thine:
And then they have their answer home.

[1] Herbert's apology for the huge change in his life, from Public Orator
at Cambridge and worldly aristocrat to simple parish priest.

GIDDINESSE

Oh, what a thing is man! how farre from power,
       From setled peace and rest!
He is some twentie sev'rall men at least
       Each sev'rall houre.

One while he counts of heav'n, as of his treasure:
       But then a thought creeps in,
And calls him coward, who for fear of sinne
       Will lose a pleasure.

Now he will fight it out, and to the warres;
       Now eat his bread in peace,
And snudge in quiet: now he scorns increase;
       Now all day spares.

He builds a house, which quickly down must go,
       As if a whirlwinde blew
And crusht the building: and it's partly true,
       His minde is so.

Oh what a sight were Man, if his attires
       Did alter with his minde;
And like a Dolphine skinne[1], his clothes combin'd
       With his desires!

[1] Dolphins were confused with dorados, a fish which went through colour changes when dying. Byron wrote:

> Parting day
> Dies like the Dolphin, whom each pang imbues
> With a new colour . . .
> The last still loveliest.

[95]

Surely if each one saw anothers heart,
      There would be no commerce,
No sale or bargain passe: all would disperse,
      And live apart.

Lord, mend or rather make us: one creation
      Will not suffice our turn:
Except thou make us dayly, we shall spurn
      Our own salvation.

THE PULLEY

When God at first made man,
Having a glasse of blessings standing by;
Let us (said he) poure on him all we can:
Let the worlds riches, which dispersed lie,
     Contract into a span.

So strength first made a way;
Then beautie flow'd, then wisdome, honour, pleasure:
When almost all was out, God made a stay,
Perceiving that alone of all his treasure
     Rest in the bottome lay.

For if I should (said he)
Bestow this jewell also on my creature,
He would adore my gifts in stead of me,
And rest in Nature, not the God of Nature:
     So both shoud losers be.

Yet let him keep the rest,
But keep them with repining restlessnesse:
Let him be rich and wearie, that at least,
If goodnesse leade him not, yet wearinesse
     May tosse him to my breast.

REDEMPTION

Having been tenant long to a rich Lord,
 Not thriving, I resolved to be bold,
 And make a suit unto him, to afford
A new small-rented lease, and cancell th' old.

In heaven at his manour I him sought:
 They told me there, that he was lately gone
 About some land, which he had dearly bought
Long since on earth, to take possession.

I straight return'd, and knowing his great birth,
 Sought him accordingly in great resorts;
 In cities, theatres, gardens, parks, and courts:
At length I heard a ragged noise and mirth

 Of theeves and murderers: there I him espied,
 Who straight, *Your suit is granted*, said, & died.

GRATEFULNESSE

Thou that hast giv'n so much to me,
Give one thing more, a gratefull heart.
See how thy beggar works on thee
          By art.

He makes thy gifts occasion more,
And sayes, If he in this be crost,
All thou hast given him heretofore
          Is lost.

But thou didst reckon, when at first
Thy word our hearts and hands did crave,
What it would come to at the worst
          To save.

Perpetuall knockings at thy doore,
Tears sullying thy transparent rooms,
Gift upon gift, much would have more,
          And comes.

This not withstanding, thou wentst on,
And didst allow us all our noise:
Nay thou hast made a sigh and grone
          Thy joyes.

Not that thou hast not still above
Much better tunes, then grones can make;
But that these countrey-aires thy love
          Did take.

Wherefore I crie, and crie again;
And in no quiet canst thou be,
Till I a thankfull heart obtain
                    Of thee:

Not thankfull, when it pleaseth me;
As if thy blessings had spare dayes:
But such a heart, whose pulse may be
                    Thy praise.

PRAISE

King of Glorie, King of Peace,
        I will love thee;
And that love may never cease,
        I will move thee.

Thou has granted my request,
        Thou hast heard me:
Thou didst note my working breast,
        Thou hast spar'd me.

Wherefore with my utmost art
        I will sing thee,
And the cream of all my heart
        I will bring thee.

Though my sinnes against me cried,
        Thou didst cleare me;
And alone, when they replied,
        Thou didst heare me.

Sev'n whole dayes, not one in seven,
        I will praise thee.
In my heart, though not in heaven,
        I can raise thee.

Thou grew'st soft and moist with tears,
        Thou relentedst:
And when Justice call'd for fears,
        Thou dissentedst.

Small it is, in this poore sort
      To enroll thee:
Ev'n eternitie is too short
      To extoll thee.

THE CALL

Come, my Way, my Truth, my Life:
Such a Way, as gives us breath:
Such a Truth, as ends all strife:
And such a Life, as killeth death.

Come, my Light, my Feast, my Strength:
Such a Light, as shows a feast:
Such a Feast, as mends in length:
Such a Strength, as makes his guest.

Come, my Joy, my Love, my Heart:
Such a Joy, as none can move:
Such a Love, as none can part:
Such a Heart, as joyes in love.

PRAYER

Prayer the Churches banquet, Angels age,
    Gods breath in man returning to his birth,
    The soul in paraphrase, heart in pilgrimage,
The Christian plummet sounding heav'n and earth;

Engine against th' Almightie, sinners towre,
    Reversed thunder, Christ-side-piercing spear,
    The six-daies world-transposing in an houre,
A kinde of tune, which all things heare and fear;

Softenesse, and peace, and joy, and love, and blisse,
    Exalted Manna, gladnesse of the best,
    Heaven in ordinarie, man well drest,
The milkie way, the bird of Paradise,

    Church-bels beyond the starres heard, the souls
      bloud,
    The land of spices; something understood.

GRACE

My stock lies dead, and no increase
Doth my dull husbandrie improve:
O let thy graces without cease
                              Drop from above!

If still the sunne should hide his face,
Thy house would but a dungeon prove,
Thy works nights captives: O let grace
                              Drop from above!

The dew doth ev'ry morning fall;
And shall the dew out-strip thy dove?
The dew, for which grasse cannot call,
                              Drop from above.

Death is still working like a mole,
And digs my grave at each remove;[1]
Let grace work too, and on my soul
                              Drop from above.

Sinne is still hammering my heart
Unto a hardnesse, void of love:
Let supplying grace, to crosse his art,
                              Drop from above.

O come! for thou dost know the way:
Or if to me thou wilt not move,
Remove me, where I need not say,
                              Drop from above.

[1] Herbert is consumptive.

VERTUE

Sweet day, so cool, so calm, so bright,
The bridall of the earth and skie:
The dew shall weep thy fall to night;
           For thou must die.

Sweet rose, whose hue angrie and brave
Bids the rash gazer wipe his eye:
Thy root is ever in its grave,
           And thou must die.

Sweet spring, full of sweet dayes and roses,
A box where sweets compacted lie;
My musick shows ye have your closes,
           And all must die.

Onely a sweet and vertuous soul,
Like season'd timber, never gives;
But though the whole world turns to coal,
           Then chiefly lives.

FROM *PROVIDENCE*

Each creature hath a wisdome for his good.
The pigeons feed their tender off-spring, crying,
When they are callow; but withdraw their food
When they are fledge, that need may teach them flying.

Bees work for man; and yet they never bruise
Their masters flower, but leave it, having done,
As fair as ever, and as fit to use;
So both the flower doth stay, and hony run.

Sheep eat the grasse, and dung the ground for more:
Trees after bearing drop their leaves for soil:
Springs vent their streams, and by expense get store:
Clouds cool by heat, and baths by cooling boil.

Who hath the vertue to expresse the rare
And curious vertues both of herbs and stones?
Is there an herb for that? O that thy care
Would show a root, that gives expressions!

And if an herb hath power, what have the starres?
A rose, besides his beauty, is a cure.
Doubtless our plagues and plentie, peace and warres
Are there much surer than our art is sure.

Thou hast hid metals: man may take them thence;
But at his perill: when he digs the place,
He makes a grave; as if the thing had sense,
And threatened man, that he should fill the space.

Ev'n poysons praise thee. Should a thing be lost?
Should creatures want for want of heed their due?
Since where are poysons, antidots are most:
The help stands close, and keeps the fear in view.

. . . And as thy house is full, so I adore
Thy curious art in marshalling thy goods.
The hills with health abound; the vales with store;
The South with marble; North with furres & woods.

. . . But who hath praise enough? nay who hath any?
None can express thy works, but he that knows them:
And none can know thy works, which are so many,
And so complete, but onely he that owes them.

CHURCH-MONUMENTS[1]

While that my soul repairs to her devotion,
Here I intombe my flesh, that it betimes
May take acquaintance of this heap of dust;
To which the blast of deaths incessant motion,
Fed with the exhalation of our crimes,
Drives all at last. Therefore I gladly trust

My bodie to this school, that it may learn
To spell his elements, and finde his birth
Written in dustie heraldrie and lines;
Which dissolution sure doth best discern,
Comparing dust with dust, and earth with earth.
These laugh at Jet, and Marble put for signes,
To sever the good fellowship of dust,
And spoil the meeting. What shall point out them,
When they shall bow, and kneel, and fall down flat
To kisse those heaps, which now they have in trust?
Deare flesh, while I do pray, learn here thy stemme
And true descent; that when thou shalt grow fat,

And wanton in thy cravings, thou mayest know,
That flesh is but the glasse, which holds the dust
That measures all our time; which also shall
Be crumbled into dust. Mark here below
How tame these ashes are, how free from lust,
That thou mayst fit thyself against thy fall.

[1] One of the great funerary poems of the seventeenth century. It reminds us that John Donne was a member of George Herbert's circle. It is thought that Herbert wrote the inscription for the tomb of his cousin Lord Danvers at Dauntsey, Wiltshire.

CHURCH-MUSICK

Sweetest of sweets, I thank you: when displeasure
    Did through my bodie wound my minde,
You took me thence, and in your house of pleasure
    A daintie lodging me assign'd.

Now I in you without a bodie move,
    Rising and falling with your wings:
We both together sweetly live and love,
    Yet say sometimes, *God help poore Kings*.[1]

Comfort, 'Ile die; for if you poste from me,
    Sure I shall do so, and much more:
But if I travell in your companie,
    You know the way to heavens doore.

---

[1] Had George Herbert been reading Shakespeare's sonnet 29?

    For thy sweet love rememb'red such wealth brings
    That then I scorn to change my state with kings.

ANTIPHON

Cho. Let all the world in ev'ry corner sing,
            My God and King.

     Vers. The heav'ns are not too high,
              His praise may thither flie:
              The earth is not too low,
              His praises there may grow.

Cho. Let all the world in ev'ry corner sing,
            My God and King.

     Vers. The church with psalms must shout,
              No doore can keep them out:
              But above all, the heart
              Must bear the longest part.

Cho. Let all the world in ev'ry corner sing,
            My God and King.

PEACE

Sweet Peace, where dost thou dwell? I humbly crave,
      Let me once know.
        I sought thee in a secret cave,
          And ask'd if Peace were there.
A hollow winde did seem to answer, No:
          Go seek elsewhere.

I did; and going did a rainbow note:
          Surely, thought I,
            This is the lace of Peaces coat:
            I will search out the matter.
But while I lookt, the clouds immediately
          Did break and scatter.

Then went I to a garden, and did spy
          A gallant flower,
            The crown Imperiall: Sure, said I,
            Peace at the root must dwell.
But when I digg'd, I saw a worm devoure
          What show'd so well.

At length I met a rev'rend good old man,
          Whom when for Peace
          I did demand; he thus began:
            There was a Prince of old[1]
At Salem dwelt, who liv'd with good increase
          Of flock and fold.

[1] Melchizedek

[112]

He sweetly liv'd; yet sweetnesse did not save
His life from foes.
But after death out of his grave
There sprang twelve stalks of wheat:[1]
Which many wondring at, got some of those
To plant and set.

It prosper'd strangely, and did soon disperse
Through all the earth:
For they that taste it do rehearse,
That vertue lies therein,
A secret vertue bringing peace and mirth
By flight of sinne.

Take of this grain[2] which in my garden grows,
And grows for you:
Make bread of it: and that repose
And peace which ev'ry where
With so much earnestnesse you do pursue,
Is onely there.

[1] The Apostles
[2] The Gospel

EVEN-SONG

Blest be the God of love
Who gave me eyes, and light, and power this day,
Both to be busie, and to play.
But much more blest be God above,

Who gave me sight alone,
Which to himself he did denie:
For when he sees my waies, I dy:
But I have got his sonne, and he hath none.

What have I brought thee home
For this thy love? have I discharg'd the debt,
Which this dayes favour did beget?
I ranne; but all I brought, was fome.

Thy diet, care, and cost
Do end in bubbles, balls of winde;
Of winde to thee whom I have crost,
But balls of wildfire to my troubled minde.

Yet still thou goest on.
And now with darknesse closest wearie eyes,
Saying to man, *It doth suffice*:
Henceforth repose; your work is done.

Thus in thy Ebony box
Thou dost inclose us, till the day
Put our amendment in our way,
And give new wheels to our disorder'd clocks.

I muse, which shows more love,
The day or night: that is the gale, this th' harbour;
That is the walk, and this the arbour;
Or that the garden, this the grove.

My God, thou art all love.
Not one poore minute scapes thy breast,
But brings a favour from above;
And in this love, more than in bed, I rest.

EASTER

Rise heart; thy Lord is risen. Sing his praise
        Without delayes,
Who takes thee by the hand, that thou likewise
        With him mayst rise:
That, as his death calcined thee to dust,
His life may make thee gold, and much more just.

Awake, my lute, and struggle for thy part
        With all thy art.
The crosse taught all wood to resound his name,
        Who bore the same.
His stretched sinews taught all strings, what key
Is best to celebrate this most high day.[1]

Consort both heart and lute, and twist a song
        Pleasant and long:
Or since all musick is but three parts vied
        And multiplied;
O let thy blessed Spirit bear a part,
And make up our defects with his sweet art.

I got me flowers to straw thy way;
I got me boughs off many a tree:
But thou wast up by break of day,
And brought'st thy sweets along with thee.

---

[1] This poem shows Herbert's musical knowledge. In Thomas
Tomkins' *Musica Deo Sacra* (1668) we learn that church music during the
seventeenth century transcended the pitch of secular music. Christ,
stretched on the cross, teaches us the high pitch by which Easter has to
be celebrated.

The Sunne arising in the East,
Though he give light, & th' East perfume;
If they should offer to contest
With thy arising, they presume.

Can there be any day but this,
Though many sunnes to shine endeavour?
We count three hundred, but we misse:
There is but one, and that one ever.

WHITSUNDAY

Listen sweet Dove unto my song,
  And spread they golden wings in me;
  Hatching my tender heart so long,
Till it get wing, and flie away with thee.

  Where is that fire which once descended
  On thy Apostles? thou didst then
  Keep open house, richly attended,
Feasting all comers by twelve chosen men.

  Such glorious gifts thou didst bestow,
  That the earth did like a heav'n appeare;
  The starres were coming down to know
If they might mend their wages, and serve here.

  The sunne, which once did shine alone,
  Hung down his head, and wisht for night,
  When he beheld twelve sunnes for one
Going about the world, and giving light.

  But since those pipes of gold, which brought
  That cordiall water to our ground,
  Were cut and martyr'd by the fault
Of those, who did themselves through their side wound

  Thou shutt'st the doore, and keep'st within:
  Scarce a good joy creeps through the chink:
  And if the braves of conqu'ring sinne
Did not excite thee, we should wholly sink.

Lord, though we change, thou art the same;
The same sweet God of love and light:
Restore this day, for thy great name,
Unto his ancient and miraculous right.

CHRISTMAS

All after pleasures as I rid one day,
   My horse and I, both tir'd, bodie and minde,
   With full crie of affections, quite astray;
I took up in the next inne I could finde.

There when I came, whom found I but my deare,
   My dearest Lord, expecting till the grief
   Of pleasures brought me to him, readie there
To be all passengers most sweet relief?

O Thou, whose glorious, yet contracted light,
   Wrapt in nights mantle, stole into a manger;
   Since my dark soul and brutish is thy right,
To Man of all beasts be not thou a stranger:

   Furnish & deck my soul, that thou mayst have
   A better lodging, then a rack[1], or grave.

The shepherds sing; and shall I silent be?
              My God, no hymne for thee?
My soul's a shepherd too; a flock it feeds
              Of thoughts, and words, and deeds.
The pasture is thy word: the streams, thy grace
              Enriching all the place.
Shepherd and flock shall sing, and all my powers
              Out-sing the day-light houres.

[1] manger

Then we will chide the sunne for letting night
            Take up his place and right:
We sing one common Lord; wherefore he should
            Himself the candle hold.
I will go searching, till I finde a sunne
            Shall stay, till we have done;
A willing shiner, that shall shine as gladly,
            As frost-nipt sunnes look sadly.
Then we will sing, and shine all our own day,
            And one another pay:
His beams shall cheer my breast, and both so twine,
Till ev'n his beams sing, and my musick shine.

THE 23RD PSALME

The God of love my shepherd is,
      And he that doth me feed:
While he is mine, and I am his,
      What can I want or need?

He leads me to the tender grasse,
      Where I both feed and rest;
Then to the streams that gently passe:
      In both I have the best.

Or if I stray, he doth convert
      And bring my minde in frame:
And all this not for my desert,
      But for his holy name.

Yea, in deaths shadie black abode
      Well may I walk, not fear:
For thou art with me; and thy rod
    To guide, thy staffe to bear.

Nay, thou didst make me sit and dine,
      Ev'n in my enemies sight;
My head with oyl, my cup with wine
      Runnes over day and night.

Surely thy sweet and wondrous love
      Shall measure all my dayes;
And as it never shall remove,
      So neither shall my praise.